MARiLEE PARRiSH

Inspiring Devotions & Prayers
for a Woman's Heart

NEVERTHELESS, SHE WAS COURAGEOUS

BARBOUR
PUBLISHING

"Be strong. Take courage. Don't be intimidated. . . . GOD, your God, is striding ahead of you. He's right there with you. He won't let you down; he won't leave you."

The words of Deuteronomy 31:6 (MSG) are packed with power! We're going to break down each phrase as we dig into this verse and see what God wants to teach us as dearly loved and valued daughters of the King.

If you have struggled with insecurity and self-doubt in the past, it's time to stop trying to muster courage from your own resources. Jesus wants to be the source of your strength and courage Himself!

Jesus, I pray a special blessing over Your beloved daughter who is reading this book. Let Your Spirit rise up in her as she seeks to know Your heart and Your will for her. I know that You won't let her down. In Your powerful name I pray. Amen.

BE STRONG

*Finally, be strong in the Lord
and in his mighty power.*
EPHESIANS 6:10 NIV

Be Strong. Toughen up. You've got this. Put on your big-girl pants. You've heard all of these (*ahem*) encouragements before, right? But do they ever help? Not so much. These types of "encouragements" are just urging you to dig down deep and find strength in yourself. But what happens when you're just plain out of strength?

The *Amplified Bible* says it this way: "Be strong in the Lord [draw your strength from Him and be empowered through your union with Him] and in the power of His [boundless] might."

Jesus encourages us to come to Him over and over. He's the living well that will never run dry. We can draw our strength from Him when ours has run out.

*Jesus, You are the mighty One.
I'm so thankful I can come to You for strength.*

JESUS HIMSELF

*I can do all things through him
who strengthens me.*

PHILIPPIANS 4:13 ESV

Job 19:25–27 (NIV) says this: "I know that my redeemer lives, and that in the end he will stand on the earth. And after my skin has been destroyed, yet in my flesh I will see God; I myself will see him with my own eyes—I, and not another. How my heart yearns within me!" Think about all the ways Jesus interacted with His disciples. He talked to them; He walked with them; and He taught them (see Luke 24:13–15). If we believe that Jesus really is alive, then He can interact with us today in powerful ways too. Jesus is the living power that gives us the strength we need each day.

Jesus, I believe You are alive and available to give me all the strength and courage I need to live my life in victory!

HOLY SPIRIT POWER

*"Do not fear [anything], for I am with you;
do not be afraid, for I am your God. I will
strengthen you, be assured I will help you;
I will certainly take hold of you with My
righteous right hand [a hand of justice,
of power, of victory, of salvation]."*

ISAIAH 41:10 AMP

If you've accepted Jesus Christ as your Savior, the power of the Holy Spirit resides within you. Either we believe this as Christians—or what is the point of our faith? In John 16:7 (ESV) Jesus says, "I tell you the truth: it is to your advantage that I go away, for if I do not go away, the Helper will not come to you. But if I go, I will send him to you."

*Jesus, thank You for sending Your Spirit to live
inside of me to teach me and give me strength.*

BE ON GUARD

Be on guard. Stand firm in the faith.
Be courageous. Be strong.
1 CORINTHIANS 16:13 NLT

Let these lyrics of the old hymn "God Will Take Care of You" by Civilla D. Martin strengthen and encourage your spirit:

Be not dismayed whate'er betide,
God will take care of you;
Beneath His wings of love abide,
God will take care of you.

The Song of Solomon 2:15 (NIV) mentions "little foxes" that come in and steal our joy and our confidence in Christ. Be on guard for that. When your heart feels heavy, take courage in the God who always helps. And then let your heart be lifted by the words of Psalm 23:6 (NIV): "Surely your goodness and love will follow me all the days of my life."

Jesus, I trust You to guard my heart.
You are so good to me.

STRENGTH FROM HIS SPIRIT

For God did not give us a spirit of timidity or cowardice or fear, but [He has given us a spirit] of power and of love and of sound judgment and personal discipline [abilities that result in a calm, well-balanced mind and self-control].

2 TIMOTHY 1:7 AMP

- - - - - - - - - - - - - - - - - - -

The Passion Translation says it this way: "For God will never give you the spirit of fear, but the Holy Spirit who gives you mighty power, love, and self-control."

If you are experiencing overwhelming fear or a sense of defeat and discouragement, you can be assured that it didn't come from God. "Perfect love casts out fear" (1 John 4:18 ESV). The Spirit that is alive in us is full of power, love, sound mind, and abilities that are beyond our own power and understanding.

*Jesus, I need strength from Your Spirit.
In Your powerful name, I cast out all fear and discouragement that come against me.*

HiS STRENGTH AND PRESENCE CONTINUALLY

Seek the LORD and his strength;
seek his presence continually!
1 CHRONICLES 16:11 ESV

God created female brains with the amazing ability to multitask. We can feed a baby, plan a grocery list, help with homework, and sign mortgage documents all at the same time without missing a beat! We also have the ability to do multiple tasks and be present with God at the same time. How are you doing at seeking the Lord during your day? Are you asking Him for courage and strength to complete your tasks? Take some time to pray, and ask God to give you a reminder that He is with you. Being a woman can be exhausting, but it doesn't have to be. Remember to rest in the strength and presence of Jesus.

Jesus, I want to seek You more than I do.
Remind me that You are with me always.

STRENGTH TO DROPOUTS

God doesn't come and go. God lasts. He's Creator of all you can see or imagine. He doesn't get tired out, doesn't pause to catch his breath. And he knows everything, inside and out. He energizes those who get tired, gives fresh strength to dropouts.
Isaiah 40:28–29 msg

Have you ever felt like a dropout of the faith? Don't beat yourself up for being human. Jesus wants you to come to Him exactly as you are and work things out with Him. God wants your heart, not your perfect behavior. If you messed up today, or even if you mess up every day, bring your messes to Jesus. There's no need to hide them, because He already knows. Ask Him to search your heart. Give Him permission to help you sort everything out.

Lord, I know that nothing I could ever do will make me more deserving of Your love and grace. You pour them over me because of Christ alone. Thank You for giving me strength.

FiRM AND IMMOVABLE

"As for the promise which I made with you when you came out of Egypt, My Spirit stands [firm and immovable] and continues with you; do not fear!"
HAGGAI 2:5 AMP

The Message paraphrase says this: " 'Yes, get to work! For I am with you.' The GOD-of-the-Angel-Armies is speaking! 'Put into action the word I covenanted with you when you left Egypt. I'm living and breathing among you right now. Don't be timid. Don't hold back.' "

The God of angel armies is your God too. He is with you and for you. He is living and breathing in you. He is firm and immovable, standing with you—always. He will never ask you to go somewhere or do something that will cause Him to leave your side.

Lord, You are the great God of angel armies. And yet You are alive and at work inside of me. That's so amazing! Thank You for never leaving my side and for bringing me courage from Your strength.

11

COMING ALIVE IN CHRIST

Death initially came by a man, and resurrection from death came by a man. Everybody dies in Adam; everybody comes alive in Christ.
1 CORINTHIANS 15:21–22 MSG

Our own strength can sometimes look and feel like death. What does that even mean? Well, have you ever used your own strength to make someone else feel small? Going toe to toe in anger with someone else is often a power struggle due to pride and sin. Confess those times to Jesus. Ask Him to humble your heart and fill you with His strength instead. Francis de Sales said, "Nothing is so strong as gentleness. Nothing so gentle as real strength." As we come alive in Christ, He fills us with the fruit of His Spirit. One of those is gentleness. Ask for it in greater measure.

Jesus, I confess my pride to You.
Wash me in Your gentle strength instead.

STRENGTH DURING TEMPTATION

*The temptations in your life are no different
from what others experience. And God is faithful.
He will not allow the temptation to be more than
you can stand. When you are tempted, he will
show you a way out so that you can endure.*

1 CORINTHIANS 10:13 NLT

Think about the things that tempt you most often:
Chocolate? Shopping? Spending too much time on social
media? We can regularly dismiss the things that tempt us
as no big deal, rationalizing that they aren't nearly as bad
as the things that tempt others, such as pornography or
things we think are "bigger" sins—and so we give in. But
overeating and spending too much can easily lead to health
and financial problems. Surrendering to temptations of any
kind really is a big deal. So what does one do? Look for the
way out. Jesus promises to always make one.

*Jesus, I surrender my temptations to You.
Show me the right way.*

WEAK IN SELF, STRONG IN CHRIST

*But he said to me, "My grace is sufficient for you,
for my power is made perfect in weakness." Therefore
I will boast all the more gladly of my weaknesses,
so that the power of Christ may rest upon me.
For the sake of Christ, then, I am content with weaknesses,
insults, hardships, persecutions, and calamities.
For when I am weak, then I am strong.*

2 CORINTHIANS 12:9–10 ESV

The apostle Paul had some sort of physical affliction (see 2 Corinthians 12:7–8). He begged God several times to take it away, but God said no. Why would He do that? Paul says that God did that for a reason. To keep him reliant on God's power instead of being conceited and proud. God promises to be with us in our limitations. How are you allowing God to shine in your areas of weakness?

*Jesus, help me to be content in my weakness,
allowing Your strength to shine through.*

VICTORY

"For the LORD your God is going with you!
He will fight for you against your enemies,
and he will give you victory!"

DEUTERONOMY 20:4 NLT

Spiritual warfare is real. The Bible tells us to be alert because our enemy prowls around looking to devour us (1 Peter 5:8). The Bible also tells us that our battles take place in the unseen world (Ephesians 6:12). Do you ever struggle with fears and worries? Fear can be a real battle for a woman, and it is one of our enemy's main schemes against us. But God has given us everything we need to overcome. We don't fight in our own strength. Take a look at Ephesians 6:10–18. Ask the Holy Spirit to teach you what you need to know to help conquer your fears. Journal about this today.

Jesus, I'm so thankful for Your provision. You see me. You know my needs. And in Your strength, I have victory!

MY STRENGTH AND SONG

*"See, God has come to save me. I will trust in him
and not be afraid. The LORD GOD is my strength
and my song; he has given me victory."*

ISAIAH 12:2 NLT

Praising and worshipping God in hard times is incredibly powerful. Praising God in times of trouble requires a leap of faith. Psalm 32:7 (NIV) says, "You are my hiding place; you will protect me from trouble and surround me with songs of deliverance." The next time you feel like running away from your problems, hide out in Jesus instead. Crank up the praise music and thank Him for His songs of deliverance. Watch and see how He makes a way for you!

*Jesus, I trust that You see me and know my heart.
I worship You during this hard time, knowing that
You've got my back and will move me forward.*

FAILING FORWARD

*My flesh and my heart may fail, but God is the rock
and strength of my heart and my portion forever.*
PSALM 73:26 AMP

Remember how we talked about digging down deep and trying to muster enough strength to get the next thing done? Sometimes our bodies and minds just give out. We mess up. We get things wrong. We fall hard. We see ourselves as failures. But God sees us through the perfect lens of Jesus. He sees us as whole and beautiful and perfect through the righteousness of Christ.

God can and will use every failure to point to His strength if you let Him. Lift your head and allow Him to lead you forward.

*Jesus, thank You that You make something beautiful
out of my mistakes. I release them into Your hands
to do the work that only You can do.*

STRENGTH WITH PEOPLE

*The Lord is my light and my salvation—
whom shall I fear? The Lord is the stronghold
of my life—of whom shall I be afraid?*

PSALM 27:1 NIV

Knowing who you are in Christ gives you supernatural strength and courage in any and every situation. If you have trouble with other people's thoughts or opinions of you or consider yourself a shy person who fears standing up for herself or others, this is great news for you! Get into God's Word and discover the truth about who you are in Christ. Ask the Holy Spirit to teach you and remind you of what God's Word says about you. You are a royal daughter of the King of all kings. You can hold your head high because you are God's child.

*Lord, when I feel less-than around certain people,
remind me that I am Yours. Give me the
courage to speak up as You lead me.*

HOPE IN THE LORD

So be strong and courageous,
all you who put your hope in the LORD!
PSALM 31:24 NLT

How do you become strong and courageous when what you actually feel is weak and afraid? You put your hope in the power and strength of the Lord. When you call on Jesus as the Lord of your life, you are declaring that He is your director, your coach, the boss of your life. You are surrendering your will to His. And when you are listening for His voice and walking in His ways, He will lead you in all the places you need to go. He will thoroughly equip and empower you for everything He wants you to do. So that means (1) you don't have to worry, and (2) He'll give you the strength you need to get the job done.

Jesus, please be the Lord over every area in my life.
My strength comes from You alone.

OUR EVER-PRESENT HELP

God is our refuge and strength,
an ever-present help in trouble.
PSALM 46:1 NIV

Self-confidence runs out eventually. Life gets tough, and even the most courageous of us gets knocked down, with little left to give it another go. But that's the very place where we find that our courage was never our own anyway. Our courage comes from Christ alone. He is our ever-present help. We can hide away in Him. And He gives us the supernatural help we need to get back up again. Read the story of Elijah today in 1 Kings 19. He was so done with life that he asked God to let him die. But God sent an angel to feed and minister to him instead. He can do the very same for you.

God, I'm so thankful that You are my ever-present
help. Please send the encouragement I need.

GOD'S PEOPLE

The LORD gives strength to his people;
the LORD blesses his people with peace.
PSALM 29:11 NIV

When you become a child of God, you are instantly granted heavenly privileges. Look them up, write them down, start believing them today:

- I am free and clean in the blood of Christ (Galatians 5:1; 1 John 1:7).
- He has rescued me from darkness and has brought me into His kingdom (Colossians 1:13).
- I have direct access to God (Ephesians 2:18).
- I am a precious child of the Father (Isaiah 43:6–7; John 1:12; Galatians 3:26).
- I am a friend of Christ (John 15:15).
- Nothing can separate me from God's love (Romans 8:38–39).
- God is for me, not against me (Romans 8:31).
- God delights in me (Psalm 149:4).
- I am God's temple (1 Corinthians 3:16).
- I am chosen by God (Colossians 3:12).

Thank You, Father!

The Master Stands by Me

At my preliminary hearing no one stood by me. They all ran like scared rabbits. But it doesn't matter—the Master stood by me and helped me spread the Message loud and clear to those who had never heard it. I was snatched from the jaws of the lion! God's looking after me, keeping me safe in the kingdom of heaven. All praise to him, praise forever! Oh, yes!

2 Timothy 4:17 MSG

When you give your life to the Master, He has your back. He will always stand by you and be with you. He will give you courage and strength to live your life with grace and truth. Have you put your trust in Him?

Jesus, I choose this day to follow You. I invite You in to be the Lord of my life. I believe that You paid for my sins and cover me with Your righteousness. Fill me with Your love and peace all the days of my life.

MY STRENGTH AND SHIELD

*The Lord is my strength and my shield; my heart
trusts in him, and he helps me. My heart leaps
for joy, and with my song I praise him.*

Psalm 28:7 NIV

When you allow Jesus to be your strength, He also becomes your shield. He is a hiding place. You can always run to Him for anything. With His mighty power, He shields you from anything coming against you. Isaiah 54:17 (NIV) says, " 'No weapon forged against you will prevail, and you will refute every tongue that accuses you. This is the heritage of the servants of the Lord, and this is their vindication from me,' declares the Lord."

*Jesus, I'm so thankful that my heritage comes from You.
You cancel attacks and assignments from the enemy
that have been sent my way. I trust that
You will shield and protect me.*

ARMED WiTH STRENGTH

*It is God who arms me with strength
and keeps my way secure.*
PSALM 18:32 NIV

- -

God arms us with strength. *The Passion Translation* of this verse says that God wraps us in power. It is through Him alone that we get our strength and power. The Bible uses a lot of imagery to connect us with God more fully. Read this verse again. Now close your eyes and picture what God is saying. Can you see Jesus arming you with strength as He wraps you in His power? What does God want you to know about this verse specifically as it pertains to you? Ask Him. He loves to speak and give clarity to His children.

*Lord, I'm so thankful for all of the ways You speak to
me. Please show me what You want me to
know about Your strength and power.*

1/9

RENEWED STRENGTH

*On the day I called, You answered me; and You made me
bold and confident with [renewed] strength in my life.*
PSALM 138:3 AMP

How many times have you started and ended a day in
exhaustion? The Lord wants to renew your strength as you
come to Him in prayer. Bring every thought and issue and
worry to Jesus and ask Him to help you sort them out.
Consider writing down all of your thoughts and feelings,
and wait in expectation for God to answer. Write down what
you hear or sense Him saying to you. Maybe a scripture, a
song, or a picture will come to mind. As you are comforted
by your beloved Father, He fills you with renewed strength
and energy to do whatever He has called you to do.

*Heavenly Father, I bring You all of the cares
on my heart. I invite You to help me sort
them out. I want to hear from You, Lord.*

1/10

THE GIVER OF POWER AND STRENGTH

Awesome is God from his sanctuary; the God of Israel—he is the one who gives power and strength to his people. Blessed be God!

PSALM 68:35 ESV

Let's pause today to just give glory to the giver of power and strength. He is the awesome God of all creation. He is worthy of all of our praise. For the next ten minutes turn on some praise music and worship Him. Thank Him for all the blessings He has given you. Thank Him for being good to you. When you worship God, even in the midst of hardship, something powerful happens as you turn your head away from yourself and gaze at Jesus. Allow Him to strengthen you through your worship time today.

Jesus, I praise You. You are Lord over my life and Lord of all. I'm so thankful for all that You have done.

GLORIOUS INNER STRENGTH

My response is to get down on my knees before the Father, this magnificent Father who parcels out all heaven and earth. I ask him to strengthen you by his Spirit—not a brute strength but a glorious inner strength—that Christ will live in you as you open the door and invite him in. And I ask him that with both feet planted firmly on love, you'll be able to take in with all followers of Jesus the extravagant dimensions of Christ's love. Reach out and experience the breadth! Test its length! Plumb the depths! Rise to the heights! Live full lives, full in the fullness of God.

EPHESIANS 3:16–19 MSG

This passage helps us more fully understand the kind of strength God offers us. It's not a brute strength, it is a glorious inner strength that shows that the Holy Spirit is alive and at work in us.

Thank You for giving me Your strength, Lord.

TAKE COURAGE

"No weapon that is formed against you will succeed;
and every tongue that rises against you in judgment
you will condemn. This [peace, righteousness, security,
and triumph over opposition] is the heritage
of the servants of the LORD, and this is their
vindication from Me," says the LORD.
ISAIAH 54:17 AMP

Have you ever lost your courage? You know, you decided you were going to do or say something because it was the right thing to do, you worked up the nerve to do it. . .and then you got nervous and backed down? This is what mustering courage in your own strength looks like. It is surface level, and when it comes under even minor attacks sometimes, it fails.

The truth is this: our heritage of courage comes from God.

Lord, I'm excited to learn more about the courage
You give me simply because I'm Your child.

FOR SUCH A TIME AS THIS

*"Who knows whether you have not come to
the kingdom for such a time as this?"*
ESTHER 4:14 ESV

God has used His people throughout history for His special plan and purpose. God's Word is full of these stories of courage. Esther was an orphan raised by her Jewish relative. And God gave her supernatural courage to save His people from annihilation. Just like Esther, God has a special purpose for you too.

Check out this quote from B. B. Warfield: "In the infinite wisdom of the Lord of all the earth, each event falls with exact precision into its proper place in the unfolding of His divine plan. Nothing, however small, however strange, occurs without His ordering, or without its particular fitness for its place in the working out of His purpose; and the end of all shall be the manifestation of His glory, and the accumulation of His praise."

*Lord, I trust that You have a great purpose for my life.
Please give me the courage I need to carry that out.*

WHY ME?

Moses answered God, "But why me? What makes you think that I could ever go to Pharaoh and lead the children of Israel out of Egypt?" "I'll be with you," God said.
EXODUS 3:11–12 MSG

Sometimes God asks His people to do hard things. But He promises to be with you *in* those hard things. Would you rather be outside of His will and in so doing be also outside of His blessing?

Scholars suggest that Moses may have had a speech impediment. He couldn't understand why God would ask *him* to go and speak to the most powerful man around and be a leader to all of Israel. You may be asking God similar questions about the hard thing He's calling you to do. Instead of worrying about what's ahead, trust God's promise for you. He will be with you.

Lord, please help me trust You in this!

WHEN GOD SAYS GO

*David replied to Abigail, "Praise the Lord, the God of Israel,
who has sent you to meet me today! Thank God for your
good sense! Bless you.... For I swear by the Lord, the God
of Israel, who has kept me from hurting you, that if you had
not hurried out to meet me, not one of Nabal's men
would still be alive tomorrow morning."*
1 SAMUEL 25:32–34 NLT

Have you ever heard the story of Abigail in the Bible?
Basically, her husband was a jerk to some important people,
and he was about to suffer dire consequences from the
future king of Israel. Abigail became aware of this, and she
sprang into action. She courageously went to David and
wisely talked him out of his plan for justice. She was a hero
to her people. Ask God for courage, like Abigail, to go when
He says to go.

Lord, help me to obey quickly when I hear Your voice.

THE LORD YOUR GOD IS WITH YOU

"Have I not commanded you? Be strong and courageous. Do not be afraid; do not be discouraged, for the Lord your God will be with you wherever you go."

JOSHUA 1:9 NIV

"Joshua fought the battle of Jericho. . . ." Does this bring a childhood Sunday school song to mind? Joshua had a big job ahead of him. It looked impossible. The Israelites finally made it into the promised land but saw that it was completely walled off. Why does everything have to be so stinkin' difficult? So God sent an angel with a command and a plan. And Joshua obeyed even when it sounded crazy (read the story!).

Joshua trusted that God would do what He said He would do. He knew God would be faithful. So when he was told to do something that seemed mighty weird, he did it anyway. And God blessed him for it.

Lord, please give me the courage to do anything You ask of me.

THE COURAGE TO RESIST

*To these four young men God gave knowledge
and understanding of all kinds of literature and
learning. And Daniel could understand
visions and dreams of all kinds.*

DANIEL 1:17 NIV

Daniel and his friends were courageous men of God. They were given courage to withstand peer pressure of all kinds. They resisted the cultural influences, and God blessed them for it. Held captive in a foreign land, they remained faithful to God and His ways. In the beginning of the book of Daniel, we see that Daniel even resisted the rich food and wine that the king had commanded for him.

We often think of courage in terms of something we need to do. But God also gives us courage to resist too. Is there anything you need courage to resist? Food? Gossip? Social media?

*God, please give me the courage to resist any temptations
that are coming against me and distracting me
from Your plan and purpose for my life.*

33

FAiTH GiVES COURAGE

*Then Nebuchadnezzar said, "Praise be to the God of
Shadrach, Meshach and Abednego, who has sent his
angel and rescued his servants! They trusted in him
and defied the king's command and were willing
to give up their lives rather than serve or
worship any god except their own God."*

DANIEL 3:28 NIV

The story of the fiery furnace is a miraculous account of faith
and courage. These three young men refused to worship
anyone but God, knowing fully that the king would have
them killed. And of course, the prideful king got angry and
had them thrown into the fire. But God came through. The
blaze was so hot that the guards who threw them in the fire
were killed, but not a hair on the young men's heads was
even singed. That's the mighty God we serve who is still
alive and well today.

*God, please fill me with the same courage to stand
up for You whenever I'm facing the fire.*

COURAGE THROUGH PRAYER

When Daniel learned that the decree had been signed and posted, he continued to pray just as he had always done. . . . Three times a day he knelt there in prayer, thanking and praising his God.

DANIEL 6:10 MSG

Daniel was an older guy when he was thrown into the lions' den. He had served God and the land of his exile faithfully over the years. He was a man of integrity, and the other governors knew it. The king wanted him to be in charge over the other lawmakers, and they didn't like that too much. So they plotted against him, even though Daniel was a good guy who had done nothing wrong. That's what started the whole lions' den fiasco. Daniel trusted his faithful God though. And no harm came to him. He was courageous because of the time he spent with God in prayer. Because he was close to God, he didn't cave to peer pressure.

Lord, what do You want to teach me in this story?

COURAGE FROM OUR MIGHTY GOD

Hezekiah rallied the people, saying, "Be strong!
Take courage! Don't be intimidated by the king of
Assyria and his troops—there are more on our side
than on their side. He only has a bunch of mere men;
we have our GOD to help us and fight for us!"
2 CHRONICLES 32:6–8 MSG

Hezekiah was facing war. The people of his land needed courage for battle. Hezekiah reminded them of who their God was. And when things looked dire, they cried out to God in prayer. And do you know what God did? He sent an angel who completely wiped out the opposing army. Just like that, it was done.

Second Chronicles 32:22 (NIV) says, "So the LORD saved Hezekiah and the people of Jerusalem. . . . He took care of them on every side." Other versions of the Bible say that God gave them rest and peace on every side.

Lord, I need some help fighting a few battles.
Please do what only You can.

REMEMBER

"GOD, who delivered me from the teeth of the lion and the claws of the bear, will deliver me from this Philistine."

1 SAMUEL 17:37 MSG

Verses 32–33 tell more of the story. " 'Master,' said David, 'don't give up hope. I'm ready to go and fight this Philistine.' "

"Saul answered David, 'You can't go and fight this Philistine. You're too young and inexperienced—and he's been at this fighting business since before you were born.' "

As you journey in faith, it becomes so important to remember God's faithfulness to you specifically. David wasn't afraid of Goliath because he remembered how God had been faithful to him in the past. Take some time to begin writing down the big things you've seen God do in your life. Write dates if you know them, or your best guess. Then commit to journaling how God shows up in your life. And when life seems hard and you need some more courage and faith, you have a black-and-white reminder of how God has been real to you.

Lord, thank You for Your great faithfulness to me.

POWERFUL AND COURAGEOUS WOMEN

Now Deborah, a prophetess, the wife of Lappidoth, was judging Israel at that time. She used to sit [to hear and decide disputes] under the palm tree of Deborah between Ramah and Bethel in the hill country of Ephraim; and the Israelites came up to her for judgment.

JUDGES 4:4–5 AMP

Deborah was a wise, God-fearing woman. People flocked to her to hear her advice. She became one of the judges over all of Israel. She urged the Jewish people to repent and turn back to God. God greatly values and uses women in ministry. God set Deborah up as a judge over all of the Jewish people, not just over other women. She commanded an army to go into battle, and God gave them victory.

God has great plans for you as a woman. Those plans are likely more than you could imagine.

Father God, I will follow where You lead, even if it seems beyond my capabilities, because You are with me.

YES, COME

But Jesus spoke to them at once. "Don't be afraid," he said.
"Take courage. I am here!" Then Peter called to him, "Lord,
if it's really you, tell me to come to you, walking on the
water." "Yes, come," Jesus said. So Peter went over the
side of the boat and walked on the water toward Jesus.
MATTHEW 14:27–29 NLT

Have you ever heard Jesus say, "Come," in a situation, so
you took a step of faith—but then you looked around and
wondered what on earth you'd done? Yep, it happens a lot.
Reality sets in and you start to sink. The great thing about
this true story is that Jesus was right there. He saw Peter's
faith, and He saw it falter. Peter was terrified after he took
his eyes off Jesus. The Bible says that "Jesus immediately
reached out and grabbed him."

Lord, I need Your rescue too. Help me keep
my eyes on You when You say, "Come."

WHEN THE SHIP GOES DOWN

"But take courage! None of you will lose your lives, even though the ship will go down. For last night an angel of the God to whom I belong and whom I serve stood beside me, and he said, 'Don't be afraid, Paul. . . . God in his goodness has granted safety to everyone sailing with you.'"
ACTS 27:22–24 NLT

Life can be so hard sometimes. We lose a loved one or a relationship, or a ministry we loved comes to an unexpected end. Sometimes the ship goes down. But God is always faithful to His people. He is with you in the storm, and He is with you when the ship goes down. Even if you were part of the cause. Psalm 34:18 (NIV) says, "The LORD is close to the brokenhearted and saves those who are crushed in spirit." When your courage has gone down with the ship, lift up your head. God is close.

Be close to me, Lord Jesus.

COURAGE TO CONFRONT

Brothers and sisters, if someone is caught in a sin,
you who live by the Spirit should restore that
person gently. But watch yourselves,
or you also may be tempted.

GALATIANS 6:1 NIV

- - - - - - - - - - - - - - - - - -

In the book of 2 Chronicles, we see King Uzziah of Judah make some poor choices. He was a good guy at first, but his power went to his head and he became prideful. He decided he was going to do something that God said not to. A courageous priest named Azariah and some others went to confront the king. But he didn't listen, and the king received major consequences from God.

It takes a lot of courage to confront someone who is actively making poor choices. It's important to be sure that God is calling you to confront someone before you take that job on yourself. Go prayerfully, humbly, and with courage from God.

Lord, help me listen for Your leading
if I am ever to confront someone.

THE COURAGE OF MOSES' MOTHER

*But when she could no longer hide him, she got a basket
made of papyrus reeds and waterproofed it with tar
and pitch. She put the baby in the basket and laid it
among the reeds along the bank of the Nile River.*

EXODUS 2:3 NLT

God gave Moses' mother the courage to put her tiny baby
boy in a waterproof basket to keep him safe in the river.
She trusted that God would care for her baby. And God did
more than she could ever imagine! Pharaoh's daughter found
the baby and ended up paying the baby's own mother to
nurse him for her. Then he grew up as royalty.

Is God asking you to trust Him in a huge way right now?
What are you afraid to give Him?

*Lord, help me release my fears and
my future into Your hands.*

GOD SHOWS UP

*"O Lord, answer me! Answer me so these people will know
that you, O Lord, are God and that you have brought them
back to yourself." Immediately the fire of the Lord flashed
down from heaven and burned up the young bull,
the wood, the stones, and the dust. It even
licked up all the water in the trench!*
1 Kings 18:37–38 nlt

Elijah didn't have any doubt in the almighty power of God.
God spoke to Elijah, and Elijah obeyed. He knew God's
voice. God told Elijah to go see King Ahab and point out
his sins. Elijah told the truth with courage and boldness
that came because he trusted God. God showed up, just
like Elijah knew He would.

Where do you need God to show up in big ways right
now? Talk to Him about this.

*Lord, please give me boldness like Elijah
and an unwavering faith in You.*

COURAGE IN TRUTH

"Do not rebel against the LORD, and don't be afraid of the people of the land. They are only helpless prey to us! They have no protection, but the LORD is with us! Don't be afraid of them!"

NUMBERS 14:9 NLT

- - - - - - - - - - - - - - - - - -

Joshua and Caleb, leaders of the Israelites, faced their people in a dangerous situation. These people who they knew well—their friends, family, and neighbors—formed an angry mob, turning on them and preparing to stone them. Joshua and Caleb pleaded with these people to return to the ways of God, but they wouldn't listen, and again God imposed dire consequences on them.

When God asks you to stand up for Him and His ways among your friends and family, He will give you the courage to speak truth in love, regardless of the way things turn out. You will be blessed for your obedience even if your words aren't valued by others.

Lord, please give me courage to speak up for Your truth.

INCREASE MY FAITH

The Lord had said to Abram, "Leave your native country,
your relatives, and your father's family, and go to the land
that I will show you. I will make you into a great nation.
I will bless you and make you famous, and you will be a
blessing to others. I will bless those who bless you and
curse those who treat you with contempt. All the
families on earth will be blessed through you."
GENESIS 12:1–3 NLT

- - - - - - - - - - - - - - - - - - - -

Can you imagine getting a directive like that from God?
What would you do? What would you struggle with the
most? Abram was told to leave everything and go. But God
was very clear, and Abram trusted that God would do what
He said. And, girl, did He! "All the families on earth" were
blessed because Abram obeyed.

Lord, I need help obeying and trusting
You more. Increase my faith, Father!

COURAGE AND OBEDIENCE

*So Noah did everything exactly
as God had commanded him.*
GENESIS 6:22 NLT

You know the story of Noah and the ark. He needed a crazy amount of courage to obey God and do what He said. God was very clear and gave Noah specific details to follow. When God wants you to obey Him, ask Him to clarify. Sometimes it will be quite obvious with specific direction from God's Word. Sometimes you will have to ask God to reveal His will for you in a certain situation or relationship. God loves to speak to His children, and He will direct you if it is truly something He wants you to do. Do you believe that? Noah obeyed God down to the most intricate details, and God blessed him for it.

*Lord, please reveal Yourself to me. Help me to know what
to do in this situation. And give me the courage to obey.*

EXTENDED PRAYER

*I answered them, "The God of heaven [has
appointed us for His purpose and] will give us success;
therefore we His servants will arise and build."*
NEHEMIAH 2:20 AMP

Nehemiah cried out to God for help in bold prayers. He heard
that his city and his friends were in trouble, and he grieved
and prayed some more. He prayed and prayed before he
acted. He received great courage from God through his
prayers, and then he went into action.

Spend some extended time with God in prayer today.
Tell Him what is on your heart, ask for His guidance, and
wait for an answer. Repent of putting God in a box, and allow
Him to speak to you in whatever way He chooses. Then arise
and do as He says.

*Lord, You are more powerful than I could ever imagine.
Forgive me for the limits I've put on You in the past.
Speak to me and give me courage to obey.*

SUPERNATURAL STRENGTH

Then the hand of the LORD came upon Elijah [giving him supernatural strength]. He girded up his loins and outran Ahab to the entrance of Jezreel [nearly twenty miles].
1 KINGS 18:46 AMP

Elijah obeyed God, but not everyone was happy with him for speaking truth and exposing their wickedness. The king's wife, Jezebel, wanted him dead. But God protected His courageous and obedient child. He gave Elijah superhuman strength and speed to outrun Ahab's horses. You may hear some Christians say that God doesn't work that way anymore. But the Bible says that God is the same yesterday, today, and forever (Hebrews 13:8 NIV). The same protector and sustainer of Elijah is your God too. He can do what He has always done and show up in powerful ways in your life.

Lord, forgive me for the times I've doubted Your power in my life. I want to know You and trust You more.

COURAGE TO START AGAIN

Then he went on alone into the wilderness, traveling all day. He sat down under a solitary broom tree and prayed that he might die. "I have had enough, LORD," he said. "Take my life, for I am no better than my ancestors who have already died." Then he lay down and slept under the broom tree. But as he was sleeping, an angel touched him and told him, "Get up and eat!"
1 KINGS 19:4–5 NLT

After all that running, Elijah collapsed, defeated. Have you ever felt like that? Like just giving up? God didn't reprimand Elijah when he was down or tell him that he just needed to have more faith. No. What did He do? He tenderly cared for him. He made a safe place for him to sleep, and then He fed him so that he would have strength and courage to start again. What a beautiful and true picture of the goodness of our God.

Thank You for Your goodness and love, Lord.

COURAGE FROM THE SOURCE

I look up to the mountains; does my strength come from mountains? No, my strength comes from God, who made heaven, and earth, and mountains. . . . God guards you from every evil, he guards your very life. He guards you when you leave and when you return, he guards you now, he guards you always.
PSALM 121:1–2, 7–8 MSG

Remember, you won't get courage by digging down deep in your own strength. Supernatural strength and courage come from God alone. He is the very source of life and power. Does this mean you can stop trying to manipulate circumstances and people to protect yourself? Yes. God is your guardian and protector. He will give you the courage and strength to do whatever it is He is asking of you. And sometimes it is simply just to rest in Him.

You are my source of courage and strength, Lord. Help me to rest in that truth.

UNTIL OUR WORK IS DONE

When I am afraid, I put my trust in you.
PSALM 56:3 NIV

George Whitefield said, "We are immortal until our work on earth is done." How does that sit with you? Take some time and mull over this quote. It takes some faith to walk that out, right? If we believe that God is who He says He is and that His Spirit is alive and at work in us, He has a specific plan and purpose for each one of us on this earth. And He will guide and protect us until our work here is done. Does that thought give you courage? If not, ask God what might be holding you back. Ask Him to shine a flashlight into your heart and mind and highlight anything He wants to redeem and set free in you.

Lord, I want to live my life with great faith and courage. Please reveal anything in me that You want to change and grow.

DON'T BE INTIMIDATED

But whoever did want him, who believed he was who he claimed and would do what he said, he made to be their true selves, their child-of-God selves.

JOHN 1:12 MSG

Have you ever seen the movie *Tangled*? Rapunzel starts getting this crazy feeling that maybe she is the lost princess! Her "mother" tries to reason with her, to talk her out of the nonsense, to completely intimidate her. But something inside her demands that she keep looking for the truth. Turns out, she really *is* the lost princess! Are you? Do you know what King Jesus says about you and the lengths He went to secure your adoption and freedom? Intimidation works when the receiver is insecure. Jesus has so much to say about your security in Him.

Jesus, show me who You really are,
so that I know who I really am too.

YOU ARE HOLY AND DEARLY LOVED

Therefore, as God's chosen people, holy and dearly loved, clothe yourselves with compassion, kindness, humility, gentleness and patience.

Colossians 3:12 niv

"God is no respecter of persons" (Acts 10:34 KJV). Other versions say that God doesn't show favoritism. There's an old saying that every man puts his pants on one leg at a time. What does all that have to do with your spiritual life? It means that God values you just as much as all the famous Christians and the heroes from the Bible. No one Christian is better or more valuable in God's kingdom than you are. Surprised? You are a dearly loved child of God, and everything you do has value and purpose in His kingdom. Not because of anything you have done or could ever do on your own, but simply because you're God's beloved daughter. God's chosen one—holy and blameless because of Jesus.

Lord, help me to believe what You say about me!

YOU BELONG BECAUSE GOD SAYS YOU DO

I want you to think about how all this makes you more significant, not less. A body isn't just a single part blown up into something huge. It's all the different-but-similar parts arranged and functioning together.
1 CORINTHIANS 12:14–15 MSG

Have you ever walked into a room and felt instantly like you didn't belong? That can happen in groups and in social settings, but it should never happen in church. Why? Because you belong there. And you belong because God says you do. As believers in Jesus Christ, we are all part of one body—the body of Christ. We all need each other to move and grow. The next time you feel intimidated or unwelcome at a church function, ask Jesus to give you courage and show you your purpose there. If you are feeling unwelcome, maybe it's because God wants you to help welcome others!

Lord, thanks for giving me a place in Your body.

YOU ARE BLAMELESS AND PURE

May God himself, the God of peace, sanctify you through and through. May your whole spirit, soul and body be kept blameless at the coming of our Lord Jesus Christ. The one who calls you is faithful, and he will do it.
1 Thessalonians 5:23–24 niv

Making mistakes is part of life. We teach this to our children, but why are we so hard on ourselves when *we* mess up? When you start criticizing or attacking yourself for making a mistake, remember the truth of who God says you are. Because of Jesus' death and resurrection, God sees you as blameless and pure. Jesus already took on all of your sin and shame, and He paid for it dearly, once and for all. So you can face any accusation, whether it's from yourself or others, with truth from God's Word.

Lord, help me to defeat any lies about myself with truth from Your Word.

YOU CAN LIFT YOUR HEAD

I sought the LORD, and he answered me; he delivered me from all my fears. Those who look to him are radiant; their faces are never covered with shame.

PSALM 34:4–5 NIV

Feeling inferior to certain people comes easily, especially when you haven't dealt with your past. Jesus came to set you free. Take a minute and look up Luke 4:18–19. There Jesus tells us why He came. Close your eyes in prayer and imagine Jesus saying these words directly to you. He came to bring *you* good news. To proclaim freedom, to give you new eyes, to set you free. He doesn't want you to be held captive by your past. What do you need Him to free in you today so that you can lift your head again?

Jesus, thank You for coming for me.
Please free me from the grip of my past.

YOU ARE CHOSEN BY GOD

"You did not choose me, but I chose you and appointed you that you should go and bear fruit and that your fruit should abide, so that whatever you ask the Father in my name, he may give it to you."

JOHN 15:16 ESV

- -

Did you know that God chose you? Yes, you. The Bible even says that He chose you before the creation of the world! Check it out: "For he chose us in him before the creation of the world to be holy and blameless in his sight" (Ephesians 1:4 NIV). Sit with that thought for a minute. Imagine God creating the whole world and already knowing that you, His beloved child, would be part of it. It's mind-blowing! Whenever you struggle with believing truths from God's Word, dig in. Ask God to show you why you struggle and to heal that area in your heart.

I'm so amazed that You really chose me to be Your child, Lord. Thank You!

YOU ARE ROYALTY

You are a chosen people. You are royal priests, a holy nation, God's very own possession. As a result, you can show others the goodness of God, for he called you out of the darkness into his wonderful light.

1 PETER 2:9 NLT

Can you picture yourself walking before your King? You are His princess. Ephesians 3:12 (NIV) says, "In him and through faith in him we may approach God with freedom and confidence." All because of Jesus and the price He paid to rescue, redeem, and free you. In the courts of heaven, you have a place of high honor. God will receive you with delight because He loves you so much. Nothing you could ever think or do will change that. All because of Jesus. Believe it.

Lord, I'm continually amazed at the truth of who You are and who I am in You.

YOU ARE A FRIEND OF GOD

"I no longer call you servants, because a servant does not know his master's business. Instead, I have called you friends, for everything that I learned from my Father I have made known to you."

JOHN 15:15 NIV

As a follower of Jesus, you become His friend as you grow in relationship. Jesus lets you in on things. He wants to be around you. He delights in you. The triune God comes and makes His home in you, and you can experience Him through Father, Son, and Holy Spirit. His ways are beyond anything you can fathom. It's mind-boggling to think that the creator of the universe wants to befriend you. Today, spend time in prayer asking Jesus what He thinks about your friendship. Are you a good friend? Is He? Ponder this today in prayer.

Jesus, I invite You to be my best friend.
Help me to honor You in that spot in my life.

59

YOU ARE FREE

"So if the Son sets you free, you are truly free."
JOHN 8:36 NLT

- -

"Jesus paid it all, all to Him I owe." You've heard that old hymn, right? Here's the thing: Jesus says there are no charges against you. You're free to go. He paid it all for you. The Bible says that He casts your sins into the depths of the sea and remembers them no more.

Freedom in Christ means that you don't have to carry around a heavy load of guilt. He wants you to walk in your freedom. He paid dearly for it. Jesus won't load you up with rules and guilt. That's religion—not Jesus. Dependence on Jesus brings rest and freedom (Matthew 11:28–30).

Jesus, help me to believe the truth that I am free.
I'm so thankful for the price You paid for that freedom.

YOU ARE FREE FROM CONDEMNATION

So now there is no condemnation for those who belong to Christ Jesus. And because you belong to him, the power of the life-giving Spirit has freed you from the power of sin that leads to death.

ROMANS 8:1–2 NLT

Check out these verses from *The Message*: "With the arrival of Jesus, the Messiah, that fateful dilemma is resolved. Those who enter into Christ's being-here-for-us no longer have to live under a continuous, low-lying black cloud. A new power is in operation. The Spirit of life in Christ, like a strong wind, has magnificently cleared the air, freeing you from a fated lifetime of brutal tyranny at the hands of sin and death."

No more black clouds. No more condemnation. No more guilt and shame. Instead, Jesus has cleared the air. You are free.

Jesus, I'm so thankful for all You've done for me.

YOU ARE HIDDEN WITH CHRIST IN GOD

Set your minds on things above, not on earthly things.
For you died, and your life is now hidden with Christ
in God. When Christ, who is your life, appears,
then you also will appear with him in glory.
COLOSSIANS 3:2–4 NIV

Your safety and security come from Christ alone. That's not just the hope of heaven someday. Jesus came so that you could know your security now. When you set your mind on things above, God gives you an eternal perspective of your life. You see people as eternal and things as temporary. The eternal becomes much more important right now than the material. You are covered, secure, made new, and completely safe in Christ. Now and forever. Lift your head.

Jesus, I accept the fact that I'm hidden with You.
You cover me and make me new. You give me confidence
to live this life with an eternal perspective.

GOD WILL FINISH WHAT HE STARTED IN YOU

*I am convinced and confident of this very thing,
that He who has begun a good work in you will
[continue to] perfect and complete it until the
day of Christ Jesus [the time of His return].*

PHILIPPIANS 1:6 AMP

Take hope! Don't be discouraged by where other people are on their journey. Stop judging yourself so harshly, and stop judging others too. That's for God to do. God will do what He's promised to do. He hasn't forgotten you. He doesn't just move you along on the journey, drop you off, and let you go. Nope. He has eternal plans and purpose for your life. He sees you. He will finish what He started in you. He is actively at work in you right now. Trust Him.

*Thank You for this reminder, Lord God. You are good,
and You see me. I put my trust in You alone.*

YOUR HEART IS GOD'S HOME

Then Judas (not Judas Iscariot) said, "But, Lord, why do you intend to show yourself to us and not to the world?" Jesus replied, "Anyone who loves me will obey my teaching. My Father will love them, and we will come to them and make our home with them."
JOHN 14:22–23 NIV

The disciples couldn't figure out why Jesus didn't come as a high king to take over the world. But Jesus has always been about individual relationship. He came as a personal God. He cares about every little detail of you. He wants you to know His heart that way too. He promises that He will make His home in you as you follow Him. As you pray today, think about the God of heaven coming and making your heart His home. What does that look like? How does it feel? What does it change for you?

Make my heart Your home, Lord.

YOU ARE A TEMPLE OF THE HOLY SPIRIT

Do you not know that your bodies are temples of the Holy Spirit, who is in you, whom you have received from God? You are not your own; you were bought at a price. Therefore honor God with your bodies.
1 CORINTHIANS 6:19–20 NIV

When you commit your life to Christ, His Spirit miraculously comes to live inside of you and you become a temple of the Holy Spirit. A *temple* is any place or object in which God dwells, as is the body of a Christian (1 Corinthians 6:19). Isn't that an amazing thing to read in a dictionary? So if your very own body is a place where God Himself dwells, how does that change how you view yourself?

Lord, forgive me for how I've viewed my body in the past. I commit to viewing myself and my body with new eyes.

ALiVE iN you

*For God wanted them to know that the riches and
glory of Christ are for you Gentiles, too. And this
is the secret: Christ lives in you. This gives
you assurance of sharing his glory.*

COLOSSIANS 1:27 NLT

God wants you to know that His riches and glory are for you.
He is alive in you. God wants this amazing truth to give you
the courage to do anything that He calls you to. Ask yourself
these questions today:

1. Do I believe Christ is alive in me?
2. How does this change the current challenge I
   am facing?
3. Am I believing any lies that prevent me from
   walking out this truth in my life?

*Holy Spirit, rise up in me in ways I've never seen before.
I give You permission to lead me in any way You choose.
I repent of my lack of faith. Please fill me with Your truth.*

YOU ARE SEATED WITH CHRIST IN THE HEAVENLIES

And He raised us up together with Him [when we believed], and seated us with Him in the heavenly places, [because we are] in Christ Jesus.

EPHESIANS 2:6 AMP

We all need Jesus because we've sinned so much. God could have just given up on the whole lot of us. But here's what *The Message* says: "Instead, immense in mercy and with an incredible love, he embraced us. He took our sin-dead lives and made us alive in Christ. He did all this on his own, with no help from us! Then he picked us up and set us down in highest heaven in company with Jesus, our Messiah." The Bible says that this is our *current* position, not a "when you die and go to heaven" position. This is powerful stuff!

Jesus, I believe what You say is true.
Help me to live my daily life like I believe it.

YOU ARE BORN OF GOD

Everyone who believes that Jesus is the Christ has been born of God, and everyone who loves the Father loves whoever has been born of him.

1 JOHN 5:1 ESV

The Bible has much to say about Jesus' followers being born of God. Take a look:

Yet to all who did receive him, to those who believed in his name, he gave the right to become children of God—children born not of natural descent, nor of human decision or a husband's will, but born of God (John 1:12–13 NIV).

We know that anyone born of God does not continue to sin; the One who was born of God keeps them safe, and the evil one cannot harm them (1 John 5:18 NIV).

I'm so thankful that You made me Your child, Lord God. I will follow You.

GOD IS ALWAYS WORKING EVERYTHING OUT

And we know that in all things God works for the good of those who love him, who have been called according to his purpose.

ROMANS 8:28 NIV

The Bible talks a lot about being blessed and having joy. When Jesus talked about having joy, He was talking about us having a deep understanding that He is with us and making everything right—no matter what. That means that even if things seem all wrong, you can still have joy. Why? Because of this promise from God right here in Romans: "In all things God works for the good of those who love him." You can bank on it. Even during hard times. He sees everything about us and is at work for our good.

Jesus, help me to trust that You're working everything out for my good.

YOU ARE SEALED BY GOD

Now it is God who makes both us and you stand firm in Christ. He anointed us, set his seal of ownership on us, and put his Spirit in our hearts as a deposit, guaranteeing what is to come.

2 CORINTHIANS 1:21–22 NIV

You have been sealed by God, and nothing and no one can snatch you out of His hands. John 10:28–29 (NIV) says, "I give them eternal life, and they shall never perish; no one will snatch them out of my hand. My Father, who has given them to me, is greater than all; no one can snatch them out of my Father's hand."

Say this out loud: "I am anointed. I am sealed by God. His Spirit is alive in my heart. I can stand firm in Christ."

Lord, help me believe that all of Your words are true.

MORE THAN CONQUERORS

No, in all these things we are more than conquerors through him who loved us. For I am convinced that neither death nor life, neither angels nor demons, neither the present nor the future, nor any powers, neither height nor depth, nor anything else in all creation, will be able to separate us from the love of God that is in Christ Jesus our Lord.
ROMANS 8:37–39 NIV

The truth of God's Word is staggering to those of us who believe. If Christians lived this truth out every day, if we walked in the courage that Christ says is ours, it would change everything. It *can* change everything. It *will* change everything for you—if you believe it.

Jesus, I want to walk in Your truth. Help me to live this out every day. Forgive me for my unbelief at times. Give me the courage to trust Your Word.

YOU ARE COMPLETE IN CHRIST

For in Christ lives all the fullness of God in a human body.
So you also are complete through your union with Christ,
who is the head over every ruler and authority.
COLOSSIANS 2:9–10 NLT

We hear that famous line from a romance movie: "You complete me." But God never meant for any of us to put that responsibility on another human being. It's too much for human shoulders. People will often fail us and let us down. And then what? When we make people our idols, we are often disappointed. Only Jesus has shoulders big enough to carry us. We are complete in Christ alone. When you are whole in Christ, you can be in relationship with others in healthy and loving ways, with mutual responsibility for the success of the relationship.

Lord, forgive me for when I've put too much
responsibility on the shoulders of others to
complete me. I am whole in You alone.

you've been transferred

For he has rescued us from the kingdom of darkness
and transferred us into the Kingdom of his dear Son,
who purchased our freedom and forgave our sins.
COLOSSIANS 1:13–14 NLT

When a transfer happens at a company, you move all of your belongings and yourself to a new office, sometimes a new state. You may even have a new role. This is exactly what Christ intends for you too. All of you has been transferred from darkness into the kingdom of light. You don't live and work in the dark anymore. You can't even go back to that office. You've been transferred out, and the doors have been locked. Allow the truth of this transfer to transform you. You're in a new state now. Let it give you courage.

Lord, I'm so thankful for this unimaginable transfer.
Help me walk in the light as You are in the light.

YOU BELONG TO GOD

You were bought with a price [you were actually purchased with the precious blood of Jesus and made His own]. So then, honor and glorify God with your body.
1 CORINTHIANS 6:20 AMP

Do you know anyone who has adopted a child? Or maybe you've had that blessing yourself. In most cases, an adoption costs a lot of money. Some bigger companies even offer adoption financial assistance because it is so costly. You pay for the adoption and legal fees, and by law that child is yours forever. Jesus did this very thing for you. No matter what kind of family you came from, good or bad, you have a new family now. With the absolute perfect parent who will never fail you. You belong to God forever.

Heavenly Father, I'm so blessed to be Your child. You are the perfect parent.

YOU ARE A LIGHT IN THE DARKNESS

"You are the light of [Christ to] the world. A city set on a hill cannot be hidden; nor does anyone light a lamp and put it under a basket, but on a lampstand, and it gives light to all who are in the house. Let your light shine before men in such a way that they may see your good deeds and moral excellence, and [recognize and honor and] glorify your Father who is in heaven."

MATTHEW 5:14–16 AMP

- -

God has put you in certain circumstances and areas to be His light in the darkness. Don't be intimidated when things look dark. You are right where you are for a season and a reason. Can you take your eyes off of your current gloomy circumstances and look up? Ask Jesus to brighten your light in the darkness.

*Jesus, please give me the courage
to shine Your light in the dark.*

DON'T GIVE THEM A SECOND THOUGHT

"Be strong and courageous, do not be afraid or tremble in dread before them, for it is the Lord your God who goes with you. He will not fail you or abandon you."

DEUTERONOMY 31:6 AMP

Remember our focus verse? "Be strong. Take courage. Don't be intimidated. . . . GOD, your God, is striding ahead of you. He's right there with you. He won't let you down; he won't leave you" (Deuteronomy 31:6 MSG). Spend some time in God's Word, and you'll see that He has lots to say about the intimidation or fear of man.

First John 4:4 (AMP) says, "Little children (believers, dear ones), you are of God and you belong to Him and have [already] overcome them [the agents of the antichrist]; because He who is in you is greater than he (Satan) who is in the world [of sinful mankind]."

Lord, release me from the fear of man
as I turn my gaze on You.

A TRANSFORMED MIND

Don't copy the behavior and customs of this world,
but let God transform you into a new person by changing
the way you think. Then you will learn to know God's will
for you, which is good and pleasing and perfect.

ROMANS 12:2 NLT

Your thoughts matter to God. Did you know that it's possible to direct your thoughts? If you notice that you're thinking negatively, at that very moment, purposefully switch your thoughts to focus on something positive. Over time you can create a healthy habit of positive thinking. As believers, we want to align our thoughts with the truth of God's Word. He has so much wisdom to share with us about how to think and how to relate to others. He does not want us to be intimidated by toxic people or the toxic thinking of our own selves at times.

Lord, highlight any wrong thinking in me.
Show me how to align my thoughts with Yours.

AS YOU THINK, YOU ARE

For as he thinks in his heart,
so is he [in behavior—one who manipulates].
PROVERBS 23:7 AMP

Guarding your thought life is vital. Your thoughts affect everything, and over time they will eventually become concrete substances in your brain.

Second Corinthians 10:5 (NIV) tells us to take our thoughts captive and make them obey Jesus. So how do you do that? When you have a bad thought about yourself or others, take it directly to Jesus. When you are feeling intimidated in any way, pray and ask Jesus to take that thought away and fill you with His truth. Then focus on something good. Ask Jesus to fill your mind with something that comes from Him.

Jesus, set my mind on things above.

A STEADFAST MIND

*You will keep in perfect peace those whose minds
are steadfast, because they trust in you.*

ISAIAH 26:3 NIV

- -

The *Amplified Bible* gives us more clarification on this verse:
"You will keep in perfect and constant peace the one whose
mind is steadfast [that is, committed and focused on You—
in both inclination and character], because he trusts and
takes refuge in You [with hope and confident expectation]."

When we focus our thoughts on Jesus, we can go into any
circumstance or relationship with confidence that comes
from setting our minds on things above. Will worrying about
what other people think of you keep you in perfect peace?
Nope, never. The exact opposite even. But the choice is
yours. You have free will over your thinking.

*Lord Jesus, help me choose to take my thoughts
captive. Please give me a steadfast mind.*

CHANGING DIRECTION

Finally, brothers and sisters, whatever is true, whatever is noble, whatever is right, whatever is pure, whatever is lovely, whatever is admirable—if anything is excellent or praiseworthy—think about such things.
PHILIPPIANS 4:8 NIV

It's easy to get off track and think about things we shouldn't—even when we're praying! We start off thinking about something good, and then we easily get distracted by other thoughts and people. The next time you find yourself thinking about something that isn't right, ask Jesus to step into your thoughts and change them! Just speak His name and ask Him to come to your rescue. The name of Jesus has all power in heaven and earth (Philippians 2:10), and just speaking His name can change the direction of your thoughts.

Jesus, Your name is powerful. I pray You will step in and change my thoughts to be pure and true when I'm distracted.

RELAX

*"For the Holy Spirit will teach you at
that time what you should say."*
Luke 12:12 NIV

The next time you find yourself in an intimidating situation, relax. *That sounds great,* you say, *but how? You don't know how my heart starts pounding and the sweat starts pouring when I get nervous in public.* Here's the thing: if Christ is alive in you, then He is at work. If He wants you to do or say something in a certain situation, you can trust Him to let you know. And you don't have to worry about it ahead of time. This might take some practice. Whenever you're headed into a stressful situation, be present with God the entire time. Invite Him to speak to you. Tell Him how you're feeling. Then let it rest in His hands. Trust Him.

*Lord, this kind of thing takes a lot more trust than
I feel I have. Please fill me with more faith.*

A HUGE PROMISE

*Don't worry about anything; instead, pray about
everything. Tell God what you need, and thank him
for all he has done. Then you will experience God's
peace, which exceeds anything we can understand.
His peace will guard your hearts and
minds as you live in Christ Jesus.*

PHILIPPIANS 4:6–7 NLT

When you hold worries inside of you, they can actually cause
harm to your body. God wants you to bring those fears and
worries to Him instead. He promises that when you do that,
a very powerful thing happens: He'll give you His peace. It's
a peace that doesn't really make sense to anyone else but
you and God, no matter what you're facing. He wants you
to be thankful instead of stressed, and He alone can help
you do that.

*God, I pray for Your peace to wash over me as
I bring my worries to You. Thank You for
always keeping Your promises.*

BOUNDARIES AND PERSONAL RESPONSIBILITY

Keep vigilant watch over your heart; that's where life starts. Don't talk out of both sides of your mouth; avoid careless banter, white lies, and gossip. Keep your eyes straight ahead; ignore all sideshow distractions. Watch your step, and the road will stretch out smooth before you. Look neither right nor left; leave evil in the dust.

PROVERBS 4:23–27 MSG

Setting and keeping good boundaries is a spiritual discipline. It's not your job to fix other people or keep them happy. You are responsible to God for yourself and your own choices, as is everyone else. It's okay to prayerfully say no—and also to be considerate and prayerful before you say yes too. God has a plan and purpose for you, and your yeses and nos to other people can hinder that process if you're not being vigilant.

Lord, show me how to have healthy boundaries that honor You.

STEADY ME

Provide me with the insight that comes only from your Word. Give my request your personal attention, rescue me on the terms of your promise. . . . Every order you've given is right. Put your hand out and steady me since I've chosen to live by your counsel.

PSALM 119:170–173 MSG

The Bible tells us that God gives us wisdom and insight, and that He gives it freely without finding fault (James 1:5–7). The only requirement is that you trust Him. Believe that God's will is best and that He will lead and guide you in making decisions that align with His purposes.

God wants you to hear His voice and know His will for you. He has promised in His Word that if you seek Him, you *will* find Him if you seek with all of your heart (Jeremiah 29:13).

Lord, help me come to You for wisdom and insight.
Steady my heart and mind in You alone.

A NEW NATURE

Since you have heard about Jesus and have learned the truth that comes from him, throw off your old sinful nature and your former way of life, which is corrupted by lust and deception. Instead, let the Spirit renew your thoughts and attitudes. Put on your new nature, created to be like God—truly righteous and holy.

Ephesians 4:21–24 nlt

People-pleasing, gossip, taking on the responsibility of others, caving to manipulation or manipulating others, dark thoughts—all of these are part of the old nature, the old self. But when Jesus comes alive in you, His Spirit empowers you to throw off the old nature and take your thoughts captive to the power and light of Christ. As you find yourself going back to old, destructive thought patterns, stop yourself in the moment and say the name of Jesus.

Jesus, I need Your help and power to change my thoughts.

A NEW START

But there is another power within me that is at war with my mind. This power makes me a slave to the sin that is still within me. Oh, what a miserable person I am! Who will free me from this life that is dominated by sin and death? Thank God! The answer is in Jesus Christ our Lord.
ROMANS 7:23–25 NLT

You find yourself slipping into old patterns, thinking negatively about yourself or others, feeling down—what then? Romans 7 echoes this same kind of humanness. The answer is the start of the very next chapter: "So now there is no condemnation for those who belong to Christ Jesus. And because you belong to him, the power of the life-giving Spirit has freed you from the power of sin that leads to death" (Romans 8:1–2 NLT). You can start again.

Jesus, thank You for the truth that I am not condemned. Please give me the power to start again.

ROYAL YET HUMBLE

Think of yourselves the way Christ Jesus thought of himself. He had equal status with God but didn't think so much of himself that he had to cling to the advantages of that status no matter what.

PHILIPPIANS 2:5 MSG

The truth of God's Word is that you are a daughter of the King. You are a princess. You are royalty. You are seated with Christ in the heavenlies. You do not have to be intimidated by any person or any situation, because you have the very source of power alive and at work in you. That is the truth. How does Jesus want you to wield that truth? Not by acting like you're better than others but by thinking of others and their needs first. You are royalty—but be like Jesus in humility.

Lord, help me to be a humble princess in Your kingdom.

HEAVENLY THINGS

*Therefore if you have been raised with Christ [to a
new life, sharing in His resurrection from the dead],
keep seeking the things that are above, where Christ is,
seated at the right hand of God. Set your mind and keep
focused habitually on the things above [the heavenly
things], not on things that are on the earth
[which have only temporal value].*

COLOSSIANS 3:1–2 AMP

Intimidating situations and people come at us often. You
will get lots of practice with this one. In that moment when
anxious feelings come, ask Jesus to give you a calm and a
peace that comes from focusing on Him. As the situation
unfolds or the intimidating person talks, invite Jesus to give
you an eternal perspective of the person or situation. Be on
the lookout for what He wants to show you.

*Jesus, help me to keep my eyes on You and listen
as You show me eternal perspectives.*

PROBLEM PEOPLE

*Trust in and rely confidently on the LORD
with all your heart and do not rely on
your own insight or understanding.*
PROVERBS 3:5 AMP

- -

"Hurting people hurt people." You've probably heard that saying before. When people act out of control or angry or manipulative, it's usually because they are hurting. They've been treated poorly, likely for most of their lives, and they often don't even realize that the way they are acting is wrong. Hopefully, recognizing this will help you have compassion for difficult people. Pray for them and the problems in their lives as you come into contact with them. They need to know and feel the love of Christ in their lives. You may be the first person ever to courageously point them to the life-changing love of Jesus.

*Lord, help me to view the problem people in my life
as people who need Your unconditional love.*

HAPPY HEART, JOYFUL MIND

*A happy heart is good medicine and a joyful mind
causes healing, but a broken spirit dries up the bones.*
PROVERBS 17:22 AMP

Stress is hard on a body, physically and mentally. Extended and unrelenting stress can cause heart problems and even death. God does not want us to carry all of that on our shoulders. It's too much. But life is hard, and traumatic things do happen. Does God want you just to sweep your troubles under the rug and paste on a happy, fake face? Surely not. Jesus invites you to come to Him with everything. As you give Him permission to heal your hurts and heartaches, He supernaturally gives you rest and peace. As you linger in His very presence, He fills you with His joy that brings healing.

*Jesus, I bring You my heartaches and my worries.
I want Your healing presence in my life.*

THE GREATEST COMMAND

And Jesus replied to him, " 'You shall love the Lord
your God with all your heart, and with all
your soul, and with all your mind.' "
MATTHEW 22:37 AMP

- - - - - - - - - - - - - - - - - - -

Reading this verse in other paraphrases can help us think about this scripture in new ways:

> Jesus said, " 'Love the Lord your God with all your
> passion and prayer and intelligence.' This is the
> most important, the first on any list" (MSG).

> Jesus answered him, " 'Love the Lord your God
> with every passion of your heart, with all the
> energy of your being, and with every
> thought that is within you' " (TPT).

What comes to mind when you think of loving God with your passion, prayer, intelligence, energy, and every thought? How can this help you when facing intimidating people or circumstances?

Lord, I want to follow the greatest command and love
You with every part of my being, in every situation.

WORDS AND THOUGHTS

*May these words of my mouth and this meditation
of my heart be pleasing in your sight, Lord,
my Rock and my Redeemer.*

PSALM 19:14 NIV

Your thoughts and your words are very important to God.
Take a look at what the Bible says: "A good person produces
good things from the treasury of a good heart, and an
evil person produces evil things from the treasury of an
evil heart. What you say flows from what is in your heart"
(Luke 6:45 NLT).

Basically, what goes in is what comes out. If the things
you are taking in, such as entertainment choices, social
media posts, and conversations, are honoring to God, you
are storing good things in your heart. And that's what will
come out. The opposite is also true. What are you filling your
heart and mind with?

*Lord, I want to honor You with what I'm
taking into my mind and heart.*

THE MIND OF CHRIST

*Who ever knows what you're thinking and planning except
you yourself? The same with God—except that he not only
knows what he's thinking, but he lets us in on it.*

1 CORINTHIANS 2:11–12 MSG

The *New Living Translation* paraphrases these verses: "And
we have received God's Spirit (not the world's spirit), so we
can know the wonderful things God has freely given us."

Verse 16 in *The Message* says, "Isaiah's question, 'Is there
anyone around who knows God's Spirit, anyone who knows
what he is doing?' has been answered: Christ knows, and
we have Christ's Spirit."

Why is all of this so extremely important? Because
without God's Spirit alive in us, we couldn't possibly know
or follow the ways of Christ. But because He is. . .we can!

*Lord, I'm so thankful that You've given me Your
Spirit. Without Him, I would never be able to
go against the strong pull of the world
to follow You and know Your ways.*

A CLEAN LIFE IN A DIRTY WORLD

How can a young person live a clean life? By carefully reading the map of your Word. I'm single-minded in pursuit of you; don't let me miss the road signs you've posted. I've banked your promises in the vault of my heart so I won't sin myself bankrupt.

PSALM 119:9–10 MSG

Our culture is sexualized and full of darkness. It can be so hard to remain pure in thought and action with impurity constantly staring us right in the face. Even when we're not looking for it, it comes and seeks us out! The Bible gives us hope that we, no matter how young or old, can live a pure life in the midst of the battle. When we store up the promises of God by reading and knowing the truth from His Word, we make deposits in our hearts that won't fail us.

Jesus, purify my mind and my heart with Your Word.

LETTING GO

"Do not remember the former things, or ponder the things of the past. Listen carefully, I am about to do a new thing, now it will spring forth; will you not be aware of it? I will even put a road in the wilderness, rivers in the desert."
ISAIAH 43:18–19 AMP

Like all of us, you probably have some things in your past you'd really like to forget. But heated conversations and failures often replay themselves in your mind. Jesus doesn't want you to keep carrying those burdens around. You can't fix everything, and you certainly can't fix other people. But you can fix your mind on Christ: "Forgetting what is behind and straining toward what is ahead, I press on toward the goal to win the prize for which God has called me heavenward in Christ Jesus" (Philippians 3:13–14 NIV).

Jesus, please help me let go of past failures and press on in faith.

ANSWERS

"This is GOD's Message, the God who made earth, made it livable and lasting, known everywhere as GOD: 'Call to me and I will answer you. I'll tell you marvelous and wondrous things that you could never figure out on your own.'"
JEREMIAH 33:3 MSG

When you talk to God, He wants to have a real conversation with you. Praying is not about sending a wish list to heaven. It's telling God how you feel about certain things and then listening for His answers. God answers us in lots of ways. He can speak to us through just about anything (one time He even spoke through a donkey! Look up the story here: Numbers 22:28–30). He loves to speak through His Word, through worship songs, through the love of another Jesus follower, through His creation—God's ways are limitless. The next time you pray, sit, and listen for God to answer. What is He telling you?

Help me to hear and understand Your answers, Lord.

BLAZING WITH HOLINESS

So roll up your sleeves, get your head in the game,
be totally ready to receive the gift that's coming when
Jesus arrives. Don't lazily slip back into those old grooves
of evil, doing just what you feel like doing. You didn't
know any better then; you do now. As obedient children,
let yourselves be pulled into a way of life shaped
by God's life, a life energetic and blazing with
holiness. God said, "I am holy; you be holy."
1 PETER 1:13–16 MSG

The Christian life is not a set of rules you must follow to please God. Again, that's religion. The difference in following Jesus is that His Spirit is alive in you. That's where the power comes from to live the Christian life! You don't have to muster strength on your own. Allow Jesus to shape your life the way He wants to. Holiness is only possible through His Spirit alive and at work in you.

Jesus, thank You for Your work in me!

The Courage to Be Real

Love from the center of who you are; don't fake
it. Run for dear life from evil; hold on for dear
life to good. Be good friends who love
deeply; practice playing second fiddle.
Romans 12:9–10 msg

Fake news, fake people, fake eyelashes. . .it's easy to check out when nothing around you seems real. But Jesus asks us to press in—to be *in* the world but not *of* it (John 17:14–19 niv). This means we don't subscribe to the spirit of the age or the popularity of the day. Instead, we offer up the timeless love and light of Jesus to everyone we come in contact with. We were sent into this world not to condemn people and separate ourselves from them but to love them and offer hope in the darkness. Keep on loving. Keep on speaking truth. Keep on being yourself.

Jesus, help me love others with Your love.
Help me be real so that others can
see the real You in me.

SPIRIT-FILLED LIFE

When God lives and breathes in you (and he does, as surely as he did in Jesus), you are delivered from that dead life. With his Spirit living in you, your body will be as alive as Christ's!

ROMANS 8:11 MSG

Imagine what your life would be like if you believed this in every moment—God Himself is living and breathing in you! That's exactly what the Bible tells us is true, yet many Christians don't live like it. They think we're sent here to trudge through mud and try to endure this life until we get to heaven. That is far from the truth. Jesus died and rose again to save you from sin and evil. He came to heal and restore you. Don't get trapped into believing anything else!

Jesus, I want to live out the truth I see in Your Word! You are alive in me!

GOD, YOUR GOD IS STRIDING AHEAD OF YOU

"It is the LORD who goes before you. He will be with you; he will not leave you or forsake you. Do not fear or be dismayed."

DEUTERONOMY 31:8 ESV

Think about the last time you felt fear—deep, alarming fear. What caused it? A noise in the night? A child in danger? Bring to mind a memory of fear that you've had. Why was it so troubling to you? As you begin your prayer time, ask Jesus what He wants you to know about this memory. Where was He when you were so worried? Sit with this memory in your mind and begin to pray. Ask Jesus for His truth in the situation. Write down what He tells you.

Jesus, I bring You my memories and my fears. Please increase my faith as I begin to understand that You will never leave me nor forsake me.

A GOD WHO FIGHTS, A DAD WHO CARRIES

"The LORD your God is going ahead of you.
He will fight for you, just as you saw him do in Egypt."
DEUTERONOMY 1:30 NLT

The Message paraphrases this verse this way: "GOD, your God, is leading the way; he's fighting for you. You saw with your own eyes what he did for you in Egypt; you saw what he did in the wilderness, how GOD, your God, carried you as a father carries his child, carried you the whole way until you arrived here."

Any good father, if his beloved child is in danger, will fight to free her from an enemy and carry her to safety. Our God does this too. Have you needed a champion in your life? Can you picture Jesus fighting for you and carrying you in His arms?

Thank You for being a good, good Father to me!

HAND OF BLESSING

You go before me and follow me.
You place your hand of blessing on my head.
PSALM 139:5 NLT

- -

God promises that nothing can separate us from His love when He has made us His children (Romans 8:38–39). Nothing you could do could make God love you more or less than He does right now. Mistakes never change how much God loves you. His Word tells us that He goes before us and follows us. His hand of blessing is on us. Does that make you feel secure and fully loved? God is a good Dad who always gets things right. You may have your own parent wounds that need healing. Jesus wants to heal them and bless you. Let Him parent you well, no matter how old you are. We're all in need of a parent's blessing.

Thank You for loving me more than I can imagine,
Father. Thank You for Your healing and blessing.

GOD'S HAND

"For I am the LORD your God, who takes hold of your right
hand and says to you, Do not fear; I will help you."
ISAIAH 41:13 NIV

If there is a scripture you need to have handy in times of trouble, this is it! Post it on your fridge and commit it to memory so that the Spirit of God can bring it to mind when you need to hear it most. Psalm 139:7–10 tells us that no matter where we go, His hand will guide us and hold us. Heading to the emergency room? Repeat Isaiah 41:13 and remember that God is holding your hand. Afraid of the future? Put your trust in the God who loves you and has great plans for you. Facing a problem that you cannot possibly bear? Take hold of God's mighty hand and believe that He will help you.

Father God, help me not to fear.
Take hold of my hand and guide me.

MADE LIKE US

For this reason he had to be made like them, fully human in every way, in order that he might become a merciful and faithful high priest in service to God, and that he might make atonement for the sins of the people. Because he himself suffered when he was tempted, he is able to help those who are being tempted.
HEBREWS 2:17–18 NIV

God chose to come to earth in human form to be made like us. To understand what it's like to be human. To be able to fully take our place and remove our sins. Because He was fully human while being fully God, He can help. He can comfort. Our God is not one who wants to remain as a distant high king, out of touch with the commoners. He wants a very personal relationship with each one of us. He lowered Himself to our level so that we could have personal and continual access to Him.

Thank You for becoming one of us, Jesus.
Thank You for Your comfort.

THROUGH THE WILDERNESS

To Him who led His people through the wilderness,
for His lovingkindness endures forever.
PSALM 136:16 AMP

Victor Hugo said, "Have courage for the great sorrows of life and patience for the small ones. And when you have finished your daily task, go to sleep in peace. God is awake." It may feel like you are stuck in the wilderness right now. But God is with you. Even when it seems like you can't see Him or hear Him or feel His presence. Dry and weary seasons cannot last forever. Take courage and trust that this season will pass. What does God want to show you in the midst of the wilderness? Ask Him to give you a vision for the season of time you're in right now.

Jesus, help me to have courage and patience
during this season. Increase my trust in You.
Show me that You're with me.

BEYOND YOUR IMAGINATION

*God is able to do much more than we ask
or think through His power working in us.*
EPHESIANS 3:20 NLV

The New International Version says that God can do "immeasurably more" than what you could imagine. When God's power is at work within you, the possibilities are beyond your imagination. Whatever problem you are facing right now—big or small—God cares. As you pray and think about it, don't put God in a box, assuming that there's no way out or that there is only one right answer. He is always going before you. And His response just might be beyond your understanding and your wildest imagination. Things aren't always what they seem. If you feel disappointed in God's answers to your prayers, look outside the box. God is always, always working everything out for your good.

*Lord, help me to trust that You are working
everything out in the best possible way.*

HEARING FROM JESUS

*Long ago God spoke many times and in many ways
to our ancestors through the prophets. And now in
these final days, he has spoken to us through his Son.
God promised everything to the Son as an inheritance,
and through the Son he created the universe.*

HEBREWS 1:1–2 NLT

When you look at Jesus, you get a clear picture of God. And He can speak directly to you. You may not hear an out-loud voice, but Jesus can speak to your heart as He answers your prayers and talks to you. And He will make Himself clear to you if you seek Him. In Jeremiah 29:13 (NIV), God says, "You will seek me and find me when you seek me with all your heart." Ask Jesus to speak clearly to you today. What is He saying?

*Jesus, help me to be able to hear from
You and get to know Your voice.*

HE KNOWS YOU BY NAME

The Lord said to Moses, "I will do what you have said. For you have found favor in My eyes, and I have known you by name."

EXODUS 33:17 NLV

The God who made all of creation knows your name and everything about you. He loves you just the way you are, and He set you on earth at this exact time in history for a purpose. God wants you to know Him. He wants you to know how much He loves you and tenderly cares for you.

God promises to go before you and to be with you wherever you go. Have you told God how much you love Him today? He is waiting to hear from you.

Lord, it's sometimes hard to believe that You know everything about me and love me anyway. But Your Word tells me it's true. I love You, God. Thanks for being so close to me.

PRAYING THE SCRIPTURES

Lead me in the right path, O Lord, or my enemies will conquer me. Make your way plain for me to follow.
PSALM 5:8 NLT

There is something powerful about praying God's Word. When you are wanting direction from God, here are some great prayers to guide you:

- Lead me by your truth and teach me, for you are the God who saves me. All day long I put my hope in you (Psalm 25:5 NLT).
- Teach me Your way, O Lord, and lead me on a level path (Psalm 27:11 AMP).
- Yes, You are my rock and my fortress; for Your name's sake You will lead me and guide me (Psalm 31:3 AMP).
- Send out your light and your truth; let them guide me. Let them lead me to your holy mountain, to the place where you live (Psalm 43:3 NLT).

Thank You for Your Word to lead me, Lord God.

IN EVERYTHING

Where can I go from your Spirit? Where can I flee from
your presence? If I go up to the heavens, you are there;
if I make my bed in the depths, you are there. If I rise
on the wings of the dawn, if I settle on the far side
of the sea, even there your hand will guide me,
your right hand will hold me fast.
PSALM 139:7–10 NIV

God has promised to be with you in everything. He has the
tools you need for every job and the map you need for every
journey. If He asks you to go somewhere or do something,
He'll always provide exactly what you need at the right
time. And you can count on Him to keep His promises. He
is always going before you and working everything out for
your good and His glory!

Father, thank You for providing everything
I need. I trust in Your promises.

STRENGTH FOR THE WEAK

He gives strength to the weak. And He gives power to him who has little strength. Even very young men get tired and become weak and strong young men trip and fall. But they who wait upon the Lord will get new strength. They will rise up with wings like eagles. They will run and not get tired. They will walk and not become weak.

ISAIAH 40:29–31 NLV

Could you use a large helping of God's power in your life? Who couldn't? The Bible says that those who wait for the Lord—the people who pray—will gain new strength! God gives strength and power to people who feel like they don't have any. . .if we simply come to Him in prayer and wait expectantly. Waiting for the Lord in prayer means that you expect Him to show up and keep His promises. You look for Him and you put your hope in Him.

Thank You for giving us Your strength, God.

BEING SURE

*Now faith is confidence in what we hope for
and assurance about what we do not see.*
HEBREWS 11:1 NIV

A man in the Bible needed help with his son. His boy had struggled with a major problem since he was born. The disciples tried to help, but they couldn't do anything, so the dad took the boy to Jesus. This dad had some doubts. He wanted to believe Jesus could do anything, but he wasn't quite sure yet. The dad said to Jesus, "I do believe; help me overcome my unbelief!" (Mark 9:24 NIV). That's a very valid prayer. Did Jesus heal the boy and increase the dad's faith? Yes, He did. Faith is believing in the unseen. It's trusting that God is real and that He is alive and working in our lives.

*Father, forgive me for the times I've believed that
I have to do things all by myself. Please help
my unbelief and increase my faith.*

STAY ALERT

Keep awake! Watch at all times. The devil is working against you. He is walking around like a hungry lion with his mouth open. He is looking for someone to eat. Stand against him and be strong in your faith.

1 PETER 5:8–9 NLV

Even though the enemy knows he has already been defeated by Jesus, he is still trying his best to get into your head and discourage you so you won't be able to live well for Jesus. That's why Jesus wants you to stay alert. Satan is the father of lies, so don't fall for his tricks (John 8:44). You have power in the name of Jesus to get rid of any evil you come up against (James 4:7). You don't have to be afraid, just alert. Don't focus on fearing the enemy. Focus on Jesus and His power to fight your battles!

Lord, help me to stay alert and not fall for any of the enemy's tricks.

LIVING LOVED

There is no fear in love. Perfect love puts fear out of our hearts. People have fear when they are afraid of being punished. The man who is afraid does not have perfect love. We love Him because He loved us first.

1 JOHN 4:18–19 NLV

God is not angry with you. Because He sees you through the love and sacrifice of Jesus, you can always approach Him without fear! A person who is afraid of God's punishment doesn't understand who she is in Christ. You don't have to work harder or be a better Christian to earn God's love. When you begin to believe who you are in Christ, everything changes. You start living differently. You realize how deeply loved you are, and that realization sets you free. As Jesus pours His love and His Spirit into your life, His love and power spill over into the lives of those around you.

You loved me first, Father. That's how I know what love is. I'm forever grateful.

DON'T GIVE UP

If a man does things to please the Holy Spirit, he will have life that lasts forever. Do not let yourselves get tired of doing good. If we do not give up, we will get what is coming to us at the right time.

GALATIANS 6:8–9 NLV

Quitters give up because they've run out of their own strength. They have nothing left to give, so they give up in defeat. But followers of Jesus depend on His strength. And it never runs out. Remember that His power shines through in our weakness. Allow Him to be your strength. Invite Him to give you power through His Spirit who is alive in you. Keep coming back to God every day in prayer, trusting that He is going before you.

Lord, thank You that I don't have to depend on my own strength. I'd much rather count on Yours instead.

PEACE iN THE MiDST OF PROBLEMS

Let the peace of Christ rule in your hearts,
since as members of one body you were
called to peace. And be thankful.
COLOSSIANS 3:15 NIV

When you let peace have power over your heart, it means that you have an inner calm that comes from trusting Jesus. When problems come, and they will, you trust in Jesus and His power over anything. When you get in the daily habit of praying and taking all of your problems, worries, and concerns to Jesus, you begin to experience the kind of peace that Jesus offers. When you're dealing with stress or too many things that are going on at once, turn your focus off of yourself and onto Jesus and others. Help someone else. Turn on the praise music. And thank God for His peace in your heart.

Lord, help me to focus on You daily, to look at
You and Your power instead of my problems.

ON EVERY ROAD

From now on every road you travel will
take you to GOD. *Follow the Covenant*
signs; read the charted directions.
PSALM 25:10 MSG

⬤ ⬤ ⬤ ⬤ ⬤ ⬤ ⬤ ⬤ ⬤ ⬤ ⬤ ⬤ ⬤ ⬤ ⬤ ⬤ ⬤

The *Amplified Bible* explains this scripture a bit more: "All the paths of the LORD are lovingkindness and goodness and truth and faithfulness to those who keep His covenant and His testimonies."

How could this be, you might ask, *when disaster and devastation happen all around us?* When you view life with an eternal perspective, you come to know this truth as Charles Spurgeon saw it, "If I should lose all I have, it is better that I should lose it, than have it—if God so wills. The worst calamity is the wisest and the kindest thing which could befall me—if God ordains it!"*

I trust You with my life, Lord. Help me to believe that all
of Your ways are good, loving, true, and faithful.
You are with me on every road.

*Charles Spurgeon, *Morning & Evening*, August 5th reading.

HELP AND HOPE

The Spirit of the Sovereign Lord is on me, because the Lord has anointed me to proclaim good news to the poor. He has sent me to bind up the broken-hearted, to proclaim freedom for the captives and release from darkness for the prisoners.

ISAIAH 61:1 NIV

Jesus came to heal people with hurting hearts and to set people free. When He quoted the Isaiah 61 passage, He wasn't just talking about physical conditions, like healing illnesses or freeing someone from jail. He was talking about ministering to people with broken hearts or stuck in fear. Jesus came to bring hope to anyone who needed it. Ask Jesus to show you how He can use you to bring His hope to hurting people. He'll point you in the right direction and give you courage as you go.

Jesus, please show me how I can help hurting people. Please give me courage to bring hope to others.

BELONGING TO GOD

But now the Lord Who made you, O Jacob, and He
Who made you, O Israel, says, "Do not be afraid.
For I have bought you and made you free.
I have called you by name. You are Mine!"
ISAIAH 43:1 NLV

- -

When you're feeling insecure, God wants you to remember something: no matter where you are, you are His! He knows your name, He is with you, and you never have to be afraid in new places or situations. When Jesus Himself tells you who you are, it changes everything. You are His beloved child. He paid the price for your freedom when He gave His life for you on the cross. You have direct access to the One who sees everything and knows everything. And you can be confident in every situation.

Lord, I'm so thankful that I belong to You. Help me to be
confident in the truth that You are always with me.

ETERNALLY PRESENT

*God's love, though, is ever and always, eternally present
to all who fear him, making everything right for them
and their children as they follow his Covenant
ways and remember to do whatever he said.*

PSALM 103:18 MSG

Nothing can separate us from the love of God (Romans 8:39). Nothing. Because of Jesus and His triumphant work on the cross, we will never be separated from God's love again. He is constantly going ahead of us and behind us, rewriting our story with "mercy's pen," as a popular worship song reminds us. Instead of worrying about the next dose of hardship coming your way, allow yourself to rest on the journey, viewing life as a great adventure with Jesus. He is eternally present with you, He loves you, and He is always at work in your life.

*Thank You for this great adventure, Lord. It's not
always easy, but I know You are always with me.*

PERSONAL, LOVING GOD

"Because I am GOD, your personal God, The Holy of Israel,
your Savior. I paid a huge price for you. . . . That's how
much you mean to me! That's how much I love you!
I'd sell off the whole world to get you back,
trade the creation just for you."

ISAIAH 43:4 MSG

Do you believe God loves you this much? You are of great worth to God. He would trade the whole world to get you back! He is your own personal God, with you always, going ahead of you forever. How does that make you feel? God wants your friends and family to know this too. Ask Him for courage to share His love with others.

Thank You for Your amazing love for me, God.
Please help me have the courage to love others
and to share with them where my love comes from.

A DUMB OX

When I was beleaguered and bitter, totally consumed
by envy, I was totally ignorant, a dumb ox in your
very presence. I'm still in your presence, but you've
taken my hand. You wisely and tenderly
lead me, and then you bless me.
PSALM 73:21–24 MSG

Have you ever felt like a dumb ox in certain situations? This comical word picture explains some of what we may have felt over our ignorance in the past. But once we invite Jesus to take our hand, everything changes. He tenderly leads us and fills us with His wisdom as we're able to take it in. As we grow in our relationship with Jesus, He blesses us immensely with His presence and His love. We no longer have to feel like a dumb animal. He takes away our shame and gives blessing instead.

Thank You, Jesus, for taking away all
my shame and blessing me instead.

AHEAD AND BEHIND

For the Lord will go ahead of you; yes,
the God of Israel will protect you from behind.
ISAIAH 52:12 NLT

Yes, our great God is striding ahead of us. He is before us and behind us and with us always. There are many scriptures to support this constant truth. Let this be our heartfelt prayer: "Train me, GOD, to walk straight; then I'll follow your true path. Put me together, one heart and mind; then, undivided, I'll worship in joyful fear. From the bottom of my heart I thank you, dear Lord; I've never kept secret what you're up to. You've always been great toward me—what love!" (Psalm 86:11–13 MSG).

Thank You, Lord, for all You've taught me and made
known to me from Your Word. I choose not to
live in fear because I know You are ahead of
me, behind me, and alive inside of me.

HE IS RIGHT THERE WITH YOU

The LORD is my shepherd; I shall not want.
PSALM 23:1 NKJV

- -

We're going to take a look at *The Passion Translation* to gain more meaning into the Twenty-Third Psalm. It's famous at funerals, but this psalm has great meaning and power for your everyday life. The word "shepherd" comes from the Hebrew root word *ra'ah*, which means "best friend." *The Passion Translation* says, "Yahweh is my best friend and my shepherd. I always have more than enough." Commit to staying close to your Shepherd, Jesus. He will always lead you on the right path. He will refresh and restore your life, making you strong. Pray that Jesus continues to make His voice known to you.

Jesus, thank You for caring for me like a gentle shepherd and best friend. I will follow You, Jesus. Help me to recognize You as You speak to me.

HE MAKES ME LIE DOWN

He makes me to lie down in green pastures;
He leads me beside the still waters.

PSALM 23:2 NKJV

- - - - - - - - - - - - - - - - - - -

The Passion Translation says, "He offers a resting place for me in his luxurious love. His tracks take me to an oasis of peace near the quiet brook of bliss."

It has been said that sheep need four things to be able to lie down: (1) freedom from fear; (2) freedom from friction with other sheep; (3) freedom from being tormented by pests; and (4) freedom from hunger. This was explained by a pastor who said: "The way for sheep to be free of these is to be keenly aware that the shepherd is nearby. So also can we lie down to rest because God's Spirit within us reassures us that He is aware and deeply involved in our lives."

Lord, I'm so thankful for the
peaceful rest You offer me.

RESTORING MY SOUL

He restores my soul; He leads me in the paths
of righteousness for His name's sake.

PSALM 23:3 NKJV

The Passion Translation says, "That's where he restores and revives my life. He opens before me the right path and leads me along in his footsteps of righteousness so that I can bring honor to his name." God restores us gently. He shows His deep care for us by looking for us when we are out wandering. He doesn't expect us to jump right up when we've been hurt and wounded. He carefully tends to our needs. When we're led in the paths of righteousness, we can simply let go of control and trust the Shepherd. He knows where to go to find fresh water. Are you willing to be led? In what area do you have trouble giving up control? Bring this to Jesus today.

Lord, I want restoration in my soul. Please help me
give up control and follow Your wise leading.

FEAR WILL NEVER CONQUER ME

Yea, though I walk through the valley of the shadow
of death, I will fear no evil; for You are with me;
Your rod and Your staff, they comfort me.

PSALM 23:4 NKJV

The Passion Translation says, "Even when your path takes me through the valley of deepest darkness, fear will never conquer me, for you already have! Your authority is my strength and my peace. The comfort of your love takes away my fear. I'll never be lonely, for you are near."

Fear doesn't have to conquer us, not when Jesus has conquered our hearts. His rod and staff are used to defend us from danger and comfort us. He uses His staff to draw us gently to His heart.

Lord, You are so good! I'm so thankful for Your loving care for me. I will not live in fear, for You have my heart.

127

CARING FOR ALL OF OUR NEEDS

You prepare a table before me in the presence of my enemies; You anoint my head with oil; my cup runs over.
PSALM 23:5 NKJV

- -

The Passion Translation says, "You become my delicious feast even when my enemies dare to fight. You anoint me with the fragrance of your Holy Spirit; you give me all I can drink of you until my heart overflows." In Bible times, shepherds would lead their flocks to the best grazing areas, a table of food, often in the presence of dangerous predators. But they were safe as long as the shepherd was close by. Shepherds would put oil on the sheep's head to cure them from illness and to keep bugs away. God is so good to remind us that He is our Shepherd and that He loves us and cares for us deeply.

Lord, You take care of all of my needs. Thank You!

ALL THE DAYS OF MY LIFE

Surely goodness and mercy shall follow me all the days of my life; and I will dwell in the house of the L<small>ORD</small> forever.

P<small>SALM</small> 23:6 N<small>KJV</small>

- - - - - - - - - - - - - - - - - - - -

The Passion Translation says, "So why would I fear the future? Only goodness and tender love pursue me all the days of my life. Then afterward, when my life is through, I'll return to your glorious presence to be forever with you!"

How amazing that God's goodness and love actually pursue you! Spend extended time in prayer with Him today, thanking Him for this great truth.

Lord God, I'm so amazed at what I'm learning about Your great love and care for me. You're more than a good shepherd. You are the source of life and love and joy in my life. You pursue me because You want a relationship with me. You are so, so good to me.

GOD WITH US

*"The virgin will conceive and give birth to
a son, and they will call him Immanuel"
(which means "God with us").*

MATTHEW 1:23 NIV

Jesus is Immanuel. This special name was foretold back in the Old Testament in the book of Isaiah, hundreds of years before Jesus was born (Isaiah 7:14). God had a rescue plan in place for His people. John 3:16–17 (NIV) tells us why: "For God so loved the world that he gave his one and only Son, that whoever believes in him shall not perish but have eternal life. For God did not send his Son into the world to condemn the world, but to save the world through him."

God became one of us. Immanuel. He is with you always.

*Jesus, I'm amazed that You became one of us.
Thank You for Your unimaginable sacrifice for me.*

THE ONLY WAY

Jesus said, "I am the Way and the Truth and the Life.
No one can go to the Father except by Me."
JOHN 14:6 NLV

- - - - - - - - - - - - - - - - - -

Jesus is the only true God. Acts 4:12 (NIV) tells us, "Salvation is found in no one else, for there is no other name under heaven given to mankind by which we must be saved." Jesus is all the fullness of God in human form (Colossians 2:9), and He is the image of the invisible God (Colossians 1:15). Jesus is how we can see God (John 1:18). God Himself came down to find you through Jesus. He is the Way, the Truth, and the Life.

Jesus, I believe that You are the one true God. I will follow You because You are the only way and the truth.

HE IS WITH ME

There is one body [of believers] and one Spirit—just as you were called to one hope when called [to salvation]— one Lord, one faith, one baptism, one God and Father of us all who is [sovereign] over all and [working] through all and [living] in all.

EPHESIANS 4:4–6 AMP

Repeat this to yourself: "He is with me. He is with me. He is with me."

The God of heaven is with you. Do you trust Him? Is there anything in your heart and mind right now that is having trouble with this truth? Ask Jesus to make that known to you. He wants you to live your life in victorious freedom. Even when you're facing hard times, and even when you've been scarred by betrayal and devastation, He is with you. He is going before you. He wants to heal your hurts.

Jesus, I want to believe that You are at work in me. Please make Yourself known to me.

HELD TOGETHER

He is before all things, and in him
all things hold together.
COLOSSIANS 1:17 NIV

Jesus is more powerful than anything you can imagine, and yet He loves and cares for you. He knows everything about you, and He cares about the things you're going through. Sometimes that can be hard to believe, but the Bible tells us it is true. And Jesus will show up and be very real in your life if you let Him. Are you facing a problem that feels too big or too small for God? Talk to Him about it. Tell Him how you really feel. Ask Him to help you believe that He cares about every little thing—and every big thing too. The closer you get to Jesus, the more your thoughts begin to match up with His thoughts.

Lord, I'm amazed that You truly care so much
for me. Thank You for holding me together.

HISTORY

"And he made from one man every nation of mankind to live on all the face of the earth, having determined allotted periods and the boundaries of their dwelling place, that they should seek God, and perhaps feel their way toward him and find him. Yet he is actually not far from each one of us, for 'In him we live and move and have our being.' "

ACTS 17:26–28 ESV

God knows your name and everything about you. He set you on earth at this exact time in history for a purpose. He wants you to know Him. He wants you to love Him and love others through Him. You matter greatly to God, and He has wonderful plans for your life.

Lord, I'm coming to believe the truth of Your great love for me personally. I want what You want for my life. Thank You for placing me at this spot in Your great story.

ONE SPIRIT

*But the person who is joined to the
Lord is one spirit with him.*
1 CORINTHIANS 6:17 NLT

Let these scriptures encourage you today:

*Yet for us there is but one God, the Father,
who is the source of all things, and we exist for
Him; and one Lord, Jesus Christ, by whom are
all things [that have been created], and we
[believers exist and have life and have been
redeemed] through Him (1 Corinthians 8:6 AMP).*

*God is faithful [He is reliable, trustworthy and ever
true to His promise—He can be depended on], and
through Him you were called into fellowship with
His Son, Jesus Christ our Lord (1 Corinthians 1:9 AMP).*

*Lord, You are faithful, reliable, trustworthy, and true
to Your promise. I know I can depend on You always.
I'm thankful that Your Spirit is in me and
that You've filled me with new life.*

PRAYER LIFE

He is not weak or ineffective in dealing with you, but powerful within you. For even though He was crucified in weakness [yielding Himself], yet He lives [resurrected] by the power of God [His Father]. For we too are weak in Him [as He was humanly weak], yet we are alive and well [in fellowship] with Him because of the power of God directed toward you.

2 Corinthians 13:3–4 AMP

- -

We can have a deep and meaningful prayer life because of this truth. Prayer is about relationship. Talk to God now in your heart or out loud and wait for His response. Sometimes He will point you to a scripture. Sometimes He will put a picture in your imagination. He might put a worship song in your mind. He may impress your heart with a strong idea or thought. Our Creator can speak to us in unlimited ways.

God, I believe in Your unlimited power directed toward me. I want to hear from You in any way You want to speak.

HONESTY

I pray to you, O Lord, my rock. Do not turn a deaf ear to me. For if you are silent, I might as well give up and die. Listen to my prayer for mercy as I cry out to you for help, as I lift my hands toward your holy sanctuary.

PSALM 28:1–2 NLT

You can be totally honest with God. You can't hide anything from Him anyway. Notice that the Psalms are full of brutal honesty. God is the safest place for you to share everything. He can shine His light on all your thoughts and feelings and help you work them out. Ask God to bring anything to light that needs to be discussed and worked through.

God, I am thankful that You are a safe place. Cast away my fears. I want to be totally honest with You. Help me long for You and desire to be with You every day.

EVERYTHING IS POSSIBLE

Jesus looked at them intently and said,
"Humanly speaking, it is impossible.
But with God everything is possible."
MATTHEW 19:26 NLT

— — — — — — — — — — — — — — — — —

What Jesus wants one person to do, is not necessarily the same exact thing He wants you to do. Jesus is all about relationship. He is a very personal God. He wants to be your friend and your trusted counselor. He wants you to come to Him first for advice. What do you need advice about today? Ask Jesus for help and guidance. Talk to Him like you would talk to your best friend. You can talk to Him out loud, or you can pray in your heart and mind. And writing down your prayers so you can have a reminder of how God answers is also very helpful.

> *God, I believe that everything is possible*
> *with You leading me. I trust You to equip*
> *me for whatever You're calling me to do.*

STRAIGHT FROM GOD

God, the one and only—I'll wait as long as he says.
Everything I hope for comes from him, so why not?
PSALM 62:5 MSG

As His Word promises, God is a safe place to be and you can trust Him absolutely. Thank Him for being a safe refuge for you. When you mess up and when you succeed, God is safe. He delights in you. He shares your sorrows and your joys. Allow Him to be with you in those times. Bring your successes and failures to Jesus now, and let Him love you in them. Read all of Psalm 62 in *The Message* as your prayer today.

Lord God, I believe it's true that everything I hope for comes from You. You have the answers I'm looking for. You are the source of strength that I'm needing. I bring You my successes and my failures. I don't have to perform for You. You love me no matter what.

WHEN GOD HELPS

The Lord is my strength and shield. I trust him with all my heart. He helps me, and my heart is filled with joy. I burst out in songs of thanksgiving. . . . Lead them like a shepherd, and carry them in your arms forever.
PSALM 28:7, 9 NLT

When God helps, He turns darkness and stress and sadness into joy and singing and thanksgiving! It's always a process. God values you, and He is careful with you. He leads you like a gentle shepherd carries his sheep. When you allow Him to help you work through your issues and feelings, miraculous things happen. He knows exactly what you need and how to get you from one step to the next. Picture yourself being carried in the arms of Jesus. What truth does He want you to remember forever?

Thank You for being gentle with me, Lord Jesus.

1/12

POWER AND PURPOSE

He delivered us and saved us and called us with a holy calling [a calling that leads to a consecrated life—a life set apart—a life of purpose], not because of our works [or because of any personal merit—we could do nothing to earn this], but because of His own purpose and grace [His amazing, undeserved favor] which was granted to us in Christ Jesus before the world began [eternal ages ago].

2 TIMOTHY 1:9 AMP

Jesus saves us and delivers us from our fears so that we can live a life of purpose. Ask Jesus to make His purpose for you clear. What are your gifts and talents? What stirs your heart in life-giving ways? Pray and listen as God writes this purpose on your heart. Make sure you write down any answer God is giving you. He will always confirm His truth for you if you ask Him.

Jesus, I'm so thankful that You want to replace my fears and anxieties with Your power and purpose.

UNLIMITED POWER

*And [so that you will begin to know] what the
immeasurable and unlimited and surpassing
greatness of His [active, spiritual]
power is in us who believe.*
EPHESIANS 1:19 AMP

The power of God is unlimited! Do you really believe that this truth applies to His power in your own life? Ask God to write this truth on your heart. It's a prayer He loves to answer. If you are struggling with doubt, bring that to Jesus. Ask Him if there are any lies you might be believing that could be preventing you from accepting the truth of His limitless power in your life.

*Jesus, I believe You are all powerful. You are beyond
my understanding and fully capable of taking care of
everything I need. I ask that You erase any lies the enemy
has been writing on my heart and fill me with Your truth.
I want to trust You more. Continue to be real to me.*

HEARING FROM GOD

"My sheep listen to my voice;
I know them, and they follow me."
JOHN 10:27 NLT

Have you limited the way God is "permitted" to speak to you? Consider the ways that you are comfortable hearing from God: through His Word, through a pastor, through music, through nature? Jesus respects our boundaries. If you've put boundaries, limits, and walls between you and God and what He is "allowed" to do in your life, your prayer life could be suffering. Ask God to break down and break through any walls you have built that might be creating a feeling of distance between you and God. Ask God to show Himself to you in new ways. Be open to the work of the Holy Spirit in your heart.

I don't want to put limits on You, Lord. Break down
any walls that I've created that might prevent
me from hearing from You.

THE GOOD SHEPHERD

"I am the Good Shepherd. The Good Shepherd gives His life for the sheep."
JOHN 10:11 NLV

Jesus tells us that He is our Shepherd. A good and gentle shepherd would love and care for his sheep with compassion and kindness. A shepherd needed the sheep to listen to him so they could travel to the best places for food. When the shepherd walked ahead of them, they followed him because they knew his voice. Jesus calls us His sheep, and He lovingly cares for each of us! Today's verse reminds us that our Shepherd even gave His very life for us! When we get to know His voice, we can be sure we're following someone we can trust.

Jesus, You are my loving Shepherd. I follow You because I trust You and know that I can count on You to lead me in the right direction.

WE ARE HIS SHEEP

*When he saw the crowds, he had compassion on them
because they were confused and helpless,
like sheep without a shepherd.*
MATTHEW 9:36 NLT

Sheep are born with an instinct to follow the leader. If one sheep does something dangerous or stupid, the sheep behind it usually follow. When Jesus came to earth, He saw that the people were acting like sheep without a shepherd—making bad choices and following others who were also making bad choices. Some people look at people making bad decisions and have no compassion for them. They judge them harshly and leave them to their consequences. But not Jesus. The Bible says that He had compassion on these people. He knew what caused them to make those choices. He loved them and wanted to help.

*Jesus, thank You for leading me. Help me to be the kind
of leader that has compassion and love for others.*

CLOSE TO THE SHEPHERD

*"If a man has a hundred sheep and one of them wanders
away, what will he do? Won't he leave the ninety-nine
others on the hills and go out to search for the one that
is lost? And if he finds it, I tell you the truth, he will rejoice
over it more than over the ninety-nine that didn't wander
away! In the same way, it is not my heavenly Father's
will that even one of these little ones should perish."*

MATTHEW 18:12–14 NLT

Good shepherds don't want to lose any of their sheep. You
matter so much to Jesus that if you ever go wandering off,
He'll search for you too! When we stay close to our Shepherd,
He leads us to the right places. When we wander off, we can
get lost, hurt, and confused. But Jesus will always come for us.

*Jesus, help me stay close to You.
Lead me on the right path.*

BRING YOUR PLANS TO JESUS

In all your ways know and acknowledge and recognize Him, and He will make your paths straight and smooth [removing obstacles that block your way].

PROVERBS 3:6 AMP

- -

Decision-making is not as difficult as we make it. When we forget that God wants to help us make choices, we get confused and anxious. When we leave God out of the decision-making process, it causes lots of unnecessary problems. Confess this truth to God in prayer. Ask forgiveness for the times you've left God out of the equation. Repent and ask God to help transform your thinking in this area. Listen for His voice as you go about your day, and He'll be with you, leading you in the right direction.

Lord, I trust that You care about everything I have on my schedule. I invite You to be a part of every plan and every decision. Remind me that You're here when I start to forget You.

HE WON'T LET YOU DOWN

He didn't tiptoe around God's promise asking cautiously skeptical questions. He plunged into the promise and came up strong, ready for God, sure that God would make good on what he had said.

ROMANS 4:20 MSG

If there is one thing you can count on for all eternity, it's that God will never let you down. Oh, you may think He has let you down or that He will in the future because something happened that you don't understand, but only God sees all and knows all. You can trust His character. You can trust that He is good. All the time. He doesn't have poor thoughts toward you—even when you mess up. Jesus already took all of that punishment. God is not mad at you. He is not disappointed in you. He looks on you with love because of Jesus. And He will never let you down.

I trust in Your goodness, God.

A STRONG FOUNDATION MATTERS

"Whoever hears these words of Mine and does them, will be like a wise man who built his house on rock. The rain came down. The water came up. The wind blew and hit the house. The house did not fall because it was built on rock."

MATTHEW 7:24–25 NLV

Jesus tells this story in Matthew to teach us about life as a Christian. If we build our lives on the firm foundation of Jesus, we won't fall apart when hard things happen. We trust in God! But if we don't have a solid foundation in Jesus, not knowing or believing His truth for our lives, we can fall apart when storms and bad things happen to us. Put your trust in the solid rock of Jesus. He will never let you fall!

Jesus, I know You are my strong foundation that will be with me no matter what storms come my way.

OUR SAFE PLACE

God is our safe place and our strength. He is always our help when we are in trouble. So we will not be afraid, even if the earth is shaken and the mountains fall into the center of the sea.

PSALM 46:1-2 NLV

The Bible tells us that God is our safe place. People, relationships, and circumstances change, but your safe place in God will never change. You can always count on Him to be the same. And you never have to be afraid when He is close. He wants to protect you, comfort you, and tell you how loved you are. Sometimes sitting in the quiet with God is the best way to pray. Ask Him to fill you with His love as you sit in His presence. Picture yourself climbing into God's lap and letting Him love you.

Thanks for always being a safe place for me, Father God!

TRAINING IN TRUTH

All Scripture is God-breathed and is useful for teaching, rebuking, correcting and training in righteousness.
2 TIMOTHY 3:16 NIV

The Bible tells us that our enemy, Satan, is the father of lies. He will try every trick in the book to get you to mess up. What did Jesus do when He was tempted? He told Satan the truth from God's Word. When you feel like you are being tempted to make a bad choice, ask Jesus for help. He has been there! He knows how to help you overcome. It matters to Jesus that you know there is always a way out of sin (1 Corinthians 10:13 NIV). He can help you make the right choice in the moment. When you memorize scripture, God's Spirit will help you remember those powerful words right when you need them. Start with 2 Timothy 3:16.

Jesus, when I'm tempted, help me remember Your truth.

PERFECT PEACE

"I have told you these things, so that in Me you may have [perfect] peace. In the world you have tribulation and distress and suffering, but be courageous [be confident, be undaunted, be filled with joy]; I have overcome the world." [My conquest is accomplished, My victory abiding.]
JOHN 16:33 AMP

The world God created is a beautiful place, but it's a messed up place too. We live in a fallen world, and things won't be perfect again until Jesus returns. Jesus promises us that this world will have trouble because it's not heaven. We can't expect it to be. It's time to let go of your expectations of what this world should be. Embrace the reality and goodness of God's peace and presence in the midst of a dark world.

Jesus, I want the perfect peace that only You offer. Help me embrace the reality that You are here to help me through this life with Your peace.

POWER AND LOVE

*But the Lord is the true God. He is the living God
and the King Who lives forever. . . . It is He Who made
the earth by His power, and the world by His wisdom.
By His understanding He has spread out the heavens.
When He speaks, there is a storm of waters in the heavens.
He makes the clouds rise from the ends of the earth.
He makes lightning for the rain, and brings
out the wind from His store-houses.*

JEREMIAH 10:10, 12–13 NLV

The God who loves and cares about you is the same God
who stretched out the heavens. It might be hard to believe
that you matter so much to God, but the Bible tells us it's
true. When you think about God's unlimited power and His
love for you, do you trust that God can handle anything you
have going on?

*Father, if You can speak water into existence at the
sound of Your voice, I know You can take care
of anything that comes my way.*

GOD SINGS

"The LORD your God is with you, the Mighty Warrior who saves. He will take great delight in you; in his love he will no longer rebuke you, but will rejoice over you with singing."

ZEPHANIAH 3:17 NIV

Getting to know God through reading His Word and prayer will change your life. He changes your thoughts to match His thoughts. As you get to know God, you will find that He's so much more than you ever thought possible. He is all-knowing, all-powerful, the Savior of the world—and yet the Bible tells us that He sings over us! God delights in you. He sees you through the eyes of Jesus. Nothing can make Him love you more or less. You cannot work for God's love. It just is.

Lord, I want to know Your words and Your truth for my life. I accept Your great love for me.

THE EXCHANGE LINE

To bestow on them a crown of beauty instead of ashes,
the oil of joy instead of mourning, and a garment
of praise instead of a spirit of despair.

ISAIAH 61:3 NIV

Remember the last time you were in the exchange line? That's never fun. Did you know that God likes to exchange things? Old for new, death for life, ashes for beauty, sadness for joy, despair for praise. He also exchanges our weakness for His strength. Can you picture yourself bringing everything that you need Him to exchange and laying it at Jesus' feet? What does He want to give you instead? Ask Him!

God, I'm so thankful that You can turn my darkness
into light, my sadness into joy, my ashes into beauty,
and my weakness into Your strength. Please show
me what You'd like to exchange in my life.

ANYTIME

Now that we know what we have—Jesus, this great High Priest with ready access to God—let's not let it slip through our fingers. . . . So let's walk right up to him and get what he is so ready to give. Take the mercy, accept the help.

Hebrews 4:14–16 msg

You've likely seen the movies where the common people need special permission to come into the palace and see the king or queen. They bow low before the throne and use titles of honor to show respect. Of course God will always deserve our respect, but we don't need special permission to go into His presence anymore! Because of Jesus, you have the ability to walk right up to God and talk to Him any time of the day. You don't have to cower in fear! Jesus has made everything right for you before God.

Father God, thank You for always receiving me.

COURAGE IN A MARTHA WORLD

*But the Lord said to her, "My dear Martha, you are worried
and upset over all these details! There is only one thing
worth being concerned about. Mary has discovered
it, and it will not be taken away from her."*
LUKE 10:41–42 NLT

You know the story. Martha was busy in the kitchen doing
what women "should" do. Mary was sitting at Jesus' feet.
Martha did what was expected, and Mary went against the
cultural norms to be with Jesus. This made Martha mad.
Jesus replied in love to Martha, but He also told her the
truth. Mary made the better choice. It's hard to go against
the norms and follow Jesus. Ask Jesus for courage to follow
Him even when everyone else says you're making the wrong
choice.

*Lord, please give me the courage
to be a Mary in a Martha world.*

No One Like You

There is no one like You among the gods, O Lord.
And there are no works like Yours. All the nations You
have made will come and worship before You, O Lord.
And they will bring honor to Your name. For You are
great and do great things. You alone are God.
PSALM 86:8–10 NLV

The time you spend with God will accomplish more than anything else you could ever do. Jeremiah 32:17 (ESV) says, "Ah, Lord GOD! It is you who have made the heavens and the earth by your great power and by your outstretched arm! Nothing is too hard for you." Ask God to help you believe that He can do anything! No problem is too hard, too big, or too small for God's help.

God of all creation, there is no one like You. I am so
blessed to be able to bring everything on my heart
to You in prayer and know that You want to help!

ASK AND RECEIVE

"So I say to you: Ask and it will be given to you; seek and you will find; knock and the door will be opened to you. For everyone who asks receives; the one who seeks finds; and to the one who knocks, the door will be opened."
LUKE 11:9–10 NIV

James 4:2 (NIV) says, "You do not have because you do not ask God." A lot of times we forget to bring things to God first. We try to get our needs met from other people and other things when God is just waiting for us to come to Him. We can ask for anything. And as we come to Him in prayer, He aligns our hearts with His.

Lord, please help me to come to You first with all my wants and needs. I know You want to help.

LOOK AND FIND

"You will seek me and find me when you seek me with all your heart."
JEREMIAH 29:13 NIV

What does seeking God and looking for Him with all your heart mean? Check out the following verses that help us understand:

- "I love those who love me, and those who seek me diligently find me" (Proverbs 8:17 ESV).
- "But seek first the kingdom of God and his righteousness, and all these things will be added to you" (Matthew 6:33 ESV).
- Seek the LORD and his strength; seek his presence continually! (1 Chronicles 16:11 ESV).
- Come near to God and he will come near to you (James 4:8 NIV).

As you look for God in everything, you will find that He is everywhere. He never leaves you.

*Thank You for being close to me, Lord.
Help me to look for You in everything.*

ALWAYS KNOCKING

"Look! I stand at the door and knock. If you hear my voice and open the door, I will come in, and we will share a meal together as friends."
Revelation 3:20 nlt

The Bible says we can knock on God's door and be invited in, but did you know He is knocking on your door too? Today's scripture tells us this truth. Wouldn't the game of hide-and-seek be so easy if the person who was supposed to be hiding was actually looking for you too? That's the really amazing thing—while we're looking for God, He's looking for us! He wants you to find Him. He makes it pretty simple. If you look for Him, you will find Him. That's a promise!

Jesus, I'm so thankful that You don't play games. You want to be found. Help me seek You always.

PRAYER LiFE

Very early in the morning, while it was still dark,
Jesus got up, left the house and went off
to a solitary place, where he prayed.
MARK 1:35 NIV

The Bible says that Jesus often went away to be alone with God and pray. Hopefully, you are beginning to understand how much you matter to God and why it's important to spend time with Him. As a follower of Jesus, your power and hope and strength to make it through each day comes from your time spent with God. Jesus lived a life of prayer. How can you live a life of prayer too? You invite Him into every moment of your day. You seek His thoughts when you need help. You ask for Him to give you love for others as you see people during the day.

Jesus, I invite You into every moment of my day.
Remind me that You are with me at all times.

BLESSING

Jabez cried out to the God of Israel, saying, "Oh that You would indeed bless me and enlarge my border [property], and that Your hand would be with me, and You would keep me from evil so that it does not hurt me!" And God granted his request.

1 CHRONICLES 4:10 AMP

Jabez asked God's blessing. And God gave it to him! Asking for God's blessing is something we see throughout the entire Bible. Does this mean that God will always give us everything we ask for? No, because God always sees all and knows all. Something that we think might be good for us could actually turn out pretty bad. That's why we trust God's will. Asking for God's blessing is asking for His purpose and power in your life rather than asking Him to give you everything you want. God knows best.

Lord, I trust You to bless me in whatever way You choose.

ALIVE IN CREATION

I will sing of the loving-kindness of the Lord forever.
I will make known with my mouth how faithful You are
to all people. . . . The heavens are Yours; and the earth is
Yours. You have made the world and all that is in it.
PSALM 89:1, 11 NLV

One of the simplest ways to actually see God's love is to go outside and experience His creation for yourself. You can see His handiwork in the flowers and trees in spring and summer. He reveals His majesty in the bright leaves showering down in the fall and in the blankets of snow He sends in the winter. Animals and creatures great and small know their creator. The birds God created are always singing His praises as they go about their busy tasks—and you can too. God gave you your voice to talk to Him, to tell of His great love, and to sing His praises.

Thanks for showing Your love for me through Your
creation, Father. I love to sing Your praises.

WONDERFULLY MADE

Your eyes saw me before I was put together.
And all the days of my life were written in
Your book before any of them came to be.
PSALM 139:16 NLV

Check out what the Bible says about you in Psalm 139:13–14 (NIV): "For you created my inmost being; you knit me together in my mother's womb. I praise you because I am fearfully and wonderfully made; your works are wonderful, I know that full well." Imagine Jesus putting you together before you were born. He knows everything about you, and He cares for you more than anything else in creation. The next time you're feeling down or unimportant or lonely, remember who made you and how much He loves you!

Jesus, You made me wonderfully. I accept that
and rejoice in who You made me to be.
You see me, Lord. And I love You.

THE POWER OF PRAYER

Therefore, confess your sins to one another [your false steps, your offenses], and pray for one another, that you may be healed and restored. The heartfelt and persistent prayer of a righteous man (believer) can accomplish much [when put into action and made effective by God—it is dynamic and can have tremendous power].

JAMES 5:16 AMP

Prayer is very powerful. Not only do we get to know God better when we talk to Him, but our prayers can make things happen. God's Word tells us to pray for others so that they can be healed and restored. This not only means that physical bodies can be healed, but also broken hearts can be fixed. Bring whatever is on your heart today to Jesus for healing. What friends and family members need His loving touch? Your prayers can make all the difference!

Lord, please increase my faith in the power of my prayers.

YOUR TEARS MATTER

*You have taken account of my wanderings; put my
tears in Your bottle. Are they not recorded in Your
book? Then my enemies will turn back in the day
when I call; this I know, that God is for me.*

PSALM 56:8–9 AMP

- -

God cares about the things that you care about. The Bible
says He even counts your tears and writes them down. In the
Old Testament, Jesus was referred to as the "Man of sorrows"
(Isaiah 53:3 AMP) because He was rejected by people (even
some of His own friends), and He was very familiar with
pain and sadness. Whatever you're going through, Jesus
understands because He's been there. Have you ever felt
left out or not good enough for other people? Talk to God
about it. Your tears matter to Him.

*Lord, thank You for Your promises. I'm so glad that
You are with me and You care about my heart.
Thank You for Your comfort and healing.*

IN ALL THINGS

*"You're blessed when you get your inside world—
your mind and heart—put right. Then you
can see God in the outside world."*

MATTHEW 5:8 MSG

The Bible talks a lot about being "blessed" and having joy. When Jesus talks about having joy, He's talking about a deep understanding that He is with us and making everything right—no matter what. That means that even if circumstances seem dire, you can still have joy. Why? Because of this promise from God right here: "And we know that in all things God works for the good of those who love him, who have been called according to his purpose" (Romans 8:28 NIV). Commit this verse to memory. It will come in handy every day of your life. God really is working all things out for your good, even when things seem all wrong.

*Jesus, help me to trust that You're working
everything out for my good.*

A LAVISH LOVE

*"I've loved you the way my Father has loved me.
Make yourselves at home in my love. If you keep my
commands, you'll remain intimately at home in my love."*
JOHN 15:9 MSG

Knowing that the God of the universe knows us personally and loves us lavishly brings us great joy. The definition of *lavish* is "to give without limit." First John 3:1 (NIV) says, "See what great love the Father has lavished on us, that we should be called children of God! And that is what we are!" God loves you without limit. Nothing can change that. You don't deserve it, so you can't possibly earn it. Rest in that truth.

Father, Your lavish love is astounding. I can't begin to understand how You can know everything about me and still love me without limit! I don't deserve Your love, but I'm thankful. I love You, Lord God.

WHEN YOU'RE NOT FEELIN' IT

Meanwhile, the moment we get tired in the waiting, God's Spirit is right alongside helping us along. If we don't know how or what to pray, it doesn't matter. He does our praying in and for us, making prayer out of our wordless sighs, our aching groans. He knows us far better than we know ourselves. . .and keeps us present before God.

ROMANS 8:26–27 MSG

Some days you don't feel like praying. You're not alone. Jesus is very aware of the human condition because He became one of us. God knows how you feel and why. That's why He sent His Spirit to live inside of us. To encourage us always. The Spirit of God will pray in us and for us when we don't know what to pray for. . .or when we just don't feel like it. If you are feeling this way today, just sit quietly somewhere and breathe. Ask the Holy Spirit to pray for you.

Father, I thank You for sending Your Spirit to pray for me. You knew how much I would need that.

NEW EVERY MORNING

Because of the Lord's great love we are not consumed,
for his compassions never fail. They are new
every morning; great is your faithfulness.
LAMENTATIONS 3:22–23 NIV

Popular *Anne of Green Gables* character Anne Shirley said, "Tomorrow is always fresh with no mistakes in it." What a great thought to remember. God's love never ends. His mercy is new every morning. Mercy is the true fact that God doesn't punish us as our sins deserve. He does this because of what Jesus did for us on the cross. So if you feel like you've failed a lot today, God has forgiven you. And you can go to sleep in peace tonight knowing that our great God has made a way for you through Jesus. God is always ready to give you a fresh start each morning.

Father, thank You for Your mercy and love
that never end. I'm ready for a fresh start.

HE WON'T LEAVE YOU

"Blessed be God, who has given peace to his people Israel just as he said he'd do. Not one of all those good and wonderful words that he spoke through Moses has misfired. May GOD, our very own God, continue to be with us just as he was with our ancestors—may he never give up and walk out on us. May he keep us centered and devoted to him, following the life path he has cleared, watching the signposts, walking at the pace and rhythms he laid down for our ancestors."

1 KINGS 8:57–58 MSG

God has promised never to leave you. And only He is capable of keeping that promise to you all the days of your life. Reaffirm your trust in Him today. He is worthy of it.

Lord God, I trust Your holy and powerful words to me. You are with me. I give You my life.

ETERNAL PERSPECTIVES

I will bless the LORD who guides me; even at night my heart instructs me. I know the LORD is always with me. I will not be shaken, for he is right beside me. No wonder my heart is glad, and I rejoice. My body rests in safety.
PSALM 16:7–9 NLT

With an eternal perspective, you can see problems and heartache in their proper light. Weeping may last for a little while, but joy *will* come (Psalm 30:5 NLT). Therefore you don't have to be shaken whenever trials come. Jesus is with you always. Bring any sadness or heartache to Him. Picture yourself carrying it all to Him. He wants to help carry your load. Ask Him to help you see things through His eyes.

Jesus, I bring all of my thoughts and feelings into Your presence. Please give me Your perspective. Thank You for Your constant presence in my life. I rest my heart in You.

NO MORE DARKNESS

*"I have come as Light into the world, so that everyone
who believes and trusts in Me [as Savior—all those who
anchor their hope in Me and rely on the truth of My
message] will not continue to live in darkness."*

JOHN 12:46 AMP

Jesus came to be a light in the darkness. When He shines
His light on anything, the darkness goes away. When you
allow Jesus to light up your heart, the darkness of sin goes
away too. Doesn't it always help to be holding someone
else's hand in the dark? It's not so frightening in the dark
when we know we're not alone. Jesus is the light that's with
you always too. You are never alone. When life on this earth
seems extra dark, remember that Jesus is holding on to you.

*Jesus, I'm so relieved and thankful that
I am never alone. You are always with me.*

RHYTHM OF GRACE

*"Come to me, all you who are weary
and burdened, and I will give you rest."*
MATTHEW 11:28 NIV

Sometimes life seems like a race that you can never win—and you get tired. Sometimes bone-weary. Take a look at the rest of what Jesus says here in Matthew: "I'll show you how to take a real rest. Walk with me and work with me—watch how I do it. Learn the unforced rhythms of grace. I won't lay anything heavy or ill-fitting on you. Keep company with me and you'll learn to live freely and lightly" (vv. 29–30 MSG). Your busyness matters to Jesus. He wants you to come to Him and rest in Him daily, finding a new, less-hurried, rhythm of grace.

*Jesus, please help me to find true rest and peace
in You. Help me to slow down and relax.*

NO DOUBT

*Then He said to Thomas, "Reach here with your finger,
and see My hands; and put out your hand and
place it in My side. Do not be unbelieving,
but [stop doubting and] believe."*

JOHN 20:27 AMP

- -

Jesus wants to make Himself known to you. He understands why you are the way you are, and He has great compassion for you. He is listening, and He loves you more than you could imagine. You are His child, and He will never abandon you. Even the painful things that happen in life, God will miraculously turn into good things if you trust in Him (Romans 8:28 again!). A lot of distractions will be coming at you always, trying to get you to doubt God's love for you. Ask the Holy Spirit to remind you of His amazing love whenever you start to doubt.

*God, help me never to doubt
Your amazing love for me!*

THE POWER iNSiDE you

*My children, you are a part of God's family. You have stood
against these false preachers and had power over them.
You had power over them because the One Who lives
in you is stronger than the one who is in the world.*

1 John 4:4 NLV

The King James Version says it this way: "Greater is he that is
in you, than he that is in the world." This is a powerful verse
that is great to remember and say out loud whenever you're
feeling afraid. Take a minute right now and write it down on
a sticky note. Ask the Holy Spirit to help you memorize it.
With God's power alive and at work in you, you have nothing
to be afraid of. Give thanks to God that He is with you always.

*Thank You for being with me all the time, Jesus.
You've given me everything I need to live for You.*

A LIVING HOPE

When we have learned not to give up, it shows we have stood the test. When we have stood the test, it gives us hope. Hope never makes us ashamed because the love of God has come into our hearts through the Holy Spirit Who was given to us.

ROMANS 5:4–5 NLV

- - - - - - - - - - - - - - - - - - -

Jesus is our living hope, and because of Him we can have a real-life relationship with God. Our hope of heaven never goes away, but we can also have great hope and peace right now. We don't have to wait for heaven to know Him and experience His love, joy, power, and peace. He wants to give that to you now—today! God always keeps His promises, and He will be with you always. Remember, Romans 8:28 tells us that God is always working everything out for your good, even the hard things.

God, thank You for keeping Your promises and being faithful to me always.

THE PROMISE

The Holy Spirit was given to us as a promise that we will receive everything God has for us. God's Spirit will be with us until God finishes His work of making us complete. God does this to show His shining-greatness.

EPHESIANS 1:14 NLV

- - - - - - - - - - - - - - - - - -

Sometimes it's hard for humans to keep their promises because they don't know what might happen in the future that could change their minds. But God always keeps His promises! God put His Spirit in your heart as a promise that He would start working in your heart, and He will continue to do so for the rest of your life. Philippians 1:6 (NLV) tells us that God will finish what He started in us. You never have to worry about God giving up on you—He never will!

Thank You, Lord, for filling me with Your life and hope. I trust Your promise to finish the work You've started in me.

EVEN WHEN YOU CAN'T SEE

But the basic reality of God is plain enough. Open your eyes and there it is! By taking a long and thoughtful look at what God has created, people have always been able to see what their eyes as such can't see: eternal power, for instance, and the mystery of his divine being. So nobody has a good excuse.
ROMANS 1:20 MSG

Sometimes it can be hard to believe in a God we can't see. But the Bible tells us that if we take a look at creation all around us and see the amazing things He has made (including you and all the other humans around you), we are without excuse when it comes to knowing that God is real.

Bring to mind friends or family members who don't believe in God. Pray that God would open up their eyes to see Him in creation.

Open the eyes of _____, Lord. Give me courage to share my faith with them.

CLOSER THAN YOU THINK

The eyes of the Lord are on those who do what is right and good. His ears are open to their cry.... The Lord is near to those who have a broken heart. And He saves those who are broken in spirit.

PSALM 34:15, 18 NLV

Jesus is closer than you think. When your heart is broken, He is with you. When your spirit feels crushed, God is close. God's Word says that He hears your prayers and His eyes are on you. He sees you. You are important to God, and He loves you more than you could ever imagine. Sometimes God will send someone to give you an extra-special dose of love at just the right time. Sometimes He will supernaturally warm your heart with love as you talk to Him. Be on the lookout for His love.

Jesus, open my eyes to see You more and know that You are near.

THE GREAT OUTPOURING

"And in the last days it shall be, God declares, that I will pour out my Spirit on all flesh, and your sons and your daughters shall prophesy, and your young men shall see visions, and your old men shall dream dreams."

ACTS 2:17 ESV

In the Old Testament, a prophet named Joel foretold that the Holy Spirit would be sent to us many, many years before it actually happened. This was all part of God's big plan to save His people. He knew we couldn't figure out life alone. He knew we would need a helper to teach us and lead us. So He sent His very own Spirit to live and grow inside of us. How have you seen the Spirit at work in your life over the past month?

Holy Spirit, please come alive in me so that Your love and power spread to everyone around me.

SPiRiTUALLY ALiVE

Spiritually alive, we have access to everything God's Spirit is doing, and can't be judged by unspiritual critics. Isaiah's question, "Is there anyone around who knows God's Spirit, anyone who knows what he is doing?" has been answered: Christ knows, and we have Christ's Spirit.

1 CORINTHIANS 2:15–16 MSG

When we have the Spirit of Jesus alive in us, we are being transformed. God's Word is brought to life in us, and we are able to understand things that we couldn't before—we are taught right and wrong. The ancient theologian Augustine said, "Without the Spirit we can neither love God nor keep His commandments." The Holy Spirit helps us to do both!

Jesus, I'm so thankful I don't have to do life on my own. You are giving me the power to accomplish everything You ask of me. Thank You for making me spiritually alive!

FEELING LONELY

*"For whoever does the will of my Father in heaven
is my brother and sister and mother."*

MATTHEW 12:50 ESV

Family is important to Jesus. Psalm 68:6 (NIV) tells us that "God sets the lonely in families." He made us to be in a community with other people. We learn from each other and grow and share God's love when we live in relationships with other people. God doesn't want us to be lonely. You are a child of God, so that means you are part of God's family! If you are having a hard time finding good friends right now, ask Jesus for help! He cares about your relationships and wants you to have the family of God around you to help you in this life.

*Jesus, will You help me find other believers who love
You and want to follow You? Please show me
what it means to be a part of Your family.*

REJECTION

Then Jesus asked them, "Didn't you ever read this in the Scriptures? 'The stone that the builders rejected has now become the cornerstone. This is the Lord's doing, and it is wonderful to see.'"

MATTHEW 21:42 NLT

Jesus knows exactly what it feels like to be rejected. During His earthly ministry, many people followed Him, but in the end, the religious leaders turned people against Him and sent Him to die on a cross. Even some of His friends betrayed Him. The crowds called for Jesus to be crucified. They humiliated Him. But He endured all of the mental, emotional, and physical anguish out of His deep love for us. People rejected Jesus, but God had chosen Him. Remember this the next time you feel alone or forgotten. God chose you to be His much-loved child. Jesus sees everything that is happening to you, and He understands your heart. He is with you.

Jesus, thank You for all that You endured on my behalf. Your love is astounding.

GOD KNOWS WHAT HE'S DOING

"I'll show up and take care of you as I promised and bring you back home. I know what I'm doing. I have it all planned out—plans to take care of you, not abandon you, plans to give you the future you hope for."

JEREMIAH 29:11 MSG

God wants good to come to you. He wants you to find Him and know Him personally. He wants you to know that you are never alone and that you always have access to the greatest power in the world. That's good news! Psalm 31:19 (GNT) says, "How wonderful are the good things you keep for those who honor you! Everyone knows how good you are, how securely you protect those who trust you." Following Jesus is the most important decision you can ever make. He has good plans for your life.

Jesus, I trust You with my life.

You've Got This

Guard the good deposit that was entrusted to you—guard it with the help of the Holy Spirit who lives in us.
2 TIMOTHY 1:14 NIV

- -

The Message says this: "So keep at your work, this faith and love rooted in Christ, exactly as I set it out for you. It's as sound as the day you first heard it from me. Guard this precious thing placed in your custody by the Holy Spirit who works in us." As a child of God, chosen before the foundation of the world, you've been given a special gift to guard and protect: the truth of God's saving Word. You don't have to guard this on your own, for you have the Spirit's power alive inside you. This knowledge should give you rest, not intimidation. You've got this—because He's got you!

Lord, I'm truly beginning to see that I have nothing to worry about. Your power is at work in me always.

ALL THINGS ARE POSSIBLE

*Jesus looked at them intently and said,
"Humanly speaking, it is impossible.
But with God everything is possible."*

MATTHEW 19:26 NLT

Have you ever gone through a situation that seemed absolutely impossible? Review that memory to see how God was with you and faithful to you during that time. It's important to remember the ways that God has been specifically faithful to you! Write them down. It's easy to think that God might be too busy with bigger things than to concern Himself with your issues. But nothing could be further from the truth.

Jesus, I believe that nothing is impossible with You!

THE HELPER

"But the Helper (Comforter, Advocate, Intercessor—Counselor, Strengthener, Standby), the Holy Spirit, whom the Father will send in My name [in My place, to represent Me and act on My behalf], He will teach you all things. And He will help you remember everything that I have told you."

JOHN 14:26 AMP

The Holy Spirit is our Counselor, Teacher, Comforter, and Guide—the promise that we are never alone fulfilled! The Spirit is the power of God alive inside of everyone who believes and commits to following Jesus. Through His power, we have everything we need (2 Peter 1:3). When we don't know what to do, we can ask! When we don't know what to pray, the Spirit helps (Romans 8:26)!

Come, Holy Spirit. Fill my heart with Your presence and peace. Thank You for helping me in everything and in every way.

GOD IS FAITHFUL

*God has said, "I will never leave
you or let you be alone."*
HEBREWS 13:5 NLV

No one is completely faithful all the time—that is, except Jesus. Humans are just that—human. We mess up. We make mistakes. We get things wrong sometimes. But God never does. He is faithful all the time! And He directs all His love and faithfulness toward you. He'll never forget you. He'll never give up on you. He'll never lie to you. He'll never ever stop loving you. Nothing you could ever do will change His mind about how much He loves you. God looks at you and smiles because He sees Jesus in you. You are covered in His righteousness (2 Corinthians 5:21 NIV).

*God, I'm so thankful that I'm always on Your mind
and that You always keep Your promises to me.*

ALWAYS

"Teach them to do all the things I have told you.
And I am with you always, even to the end of the world."
MATTHEW 28:20 NLV

- - - - - - - - - - - - - - - - - - - -

After Jesus conquered death and rose from the grave, He appeared many times to His followers. The last thing He had to say to them and to us before He went back to heaven is this: "I am with you always." The last thing someone says to you is usually pretty important. And this is the most important thing God wanted us to know. He is Immanuel, God with us. Always. His Spirit is alive in our hearts. Any confidence we have is flimsy at best unless it is based on the knowledge that the Spirit of Christ is alive and at work within us!

Jesus, thank You for Your great love for me.
Overwhelm me with the truth that
You are always with me.

191

BECAUSE I SET MY LOVE ON HIM

*"Because he set his love on Me, therefore I will save him;
I will set him [securely] on high, because he knows My
name [he confidently trusts and relies on Me, knowing
I will never abandon him, no, never]. He will call upon
Me, and I will answer him; I will be with him in trouble;
I will rescue him and honor him. With a long life I will
satisfy him and I will let him see My salvation."*
PSALM 91:14–16 AMP

As a precious daughter of the King, you are treasured in God's
eyes. You can bank on His promises to you: God, your God,
is striding ahead of you. He's right there with you. He won't
let you down. He won't leave you. Have courage, because
He will never abandon you, no, never!

*I love You, God. I call on Your
name because I trust You.*